SUPERMAN
R E T U R N S ™

SUPERMAN RETURNS: THE SHOOTING SCRIPT

ISBN 1 84576 332 7
ISBN-13 9781845763329

Published by
Titan Books
A division of
Titan Publishing Group Ltd
144 Southwark St
London
SE1 0UP

First edition July, 2006
10 9 8 7 6 5 4 3 2 1

Storyboards drawn by Colin Grant and Ed Natividad.

Visit our websites:
www.titanbooks.com
www.dccomics.com

Did you enjoy this book? We love to hear from our readers. Please e-mail us at:
readerfeedback@titanemail.com or write to Reader Feedback at the above address.

To subscribe to our regular newsletter for up-to-the-minute news, great offers and competitions, email: titan-news@titanemail.com

A CIP catalogue record for this title is available from the British Library.

Printed in Canada

SUPERMAN
R E T U R N S

THE COMPLETE SHOOTING SCRIPT

Screenplay by
Michael Dougherty & Dan Harris

Story by
Bryan Singer & Michael Dougherty & Dan Harris

Superman created by Jerry Siegel and Joe Shuster

TITAN BOOKS

CONTENTS

Bryan Singer

INTERVIEWED BY DAVID HUGHES

Bryan Singer achieved widespread critical and commercial success with his explosive second feature, *The Usual Suspects*, for which screenwriter Christopher McQuarrie and actor Kevin Spacey won Academy Awards. His next film, an adaptation of the Stephen King novella *Apt Pupil*, paved the way for his first comic book blockbuster, *X-Men*, followed in 2003 by *X2: X-Men United*. In between the *X-Men* films and *Superman Returns*, Singer also found the time to produce and direct the pilot episode of the hit TV series *House,* starring Hugh Laurie.

When did you first talk about the possibility of making a Superman movie?

I've always been interested in it, but there was a time when they were thinking of making *Batman vs. Superman* with [*Troy* director] Wolfgang Petersen, and I started to talk about what would you do with that, who would be the villain – I guess Batman would be the villain, but he couldn't really be a serious villain, so he'd have to be redeemable at some point. But I always had a notion for a Superman film – that Superman would be gone somewhere and then would return, and there were a few other aspects of the story that I had pitched to Richard Donner and his wife [*X-Men* producer Lauren Shuler Donner] in a hotel room one day during publicity for *X-Men 2*. We'd had some conversations during the making of the first *X-Men*, but it was at this point that I told Richard Donner that if I could ever make a Superman movie I wouldn't remake his film, but make a kind of sequel in a strange, vague sense. I would put that film in history, and Superman would be gone for a period of time and then come back, and the world would have moved on without him. I didn't talk about the family at that point. But Dick thought that was a wonderful idea, and just the notion of me doing it, and I got a sense from him that I had his blessing – that's the short version.

Wasn't even the idea of making a new Superman film intimidating, given that Richard Donner had made such a great film?

I agree with you 100%. I can watch *Superman: The Movie*, particularly parts of it, many, many times. In fact, I'm producing a documentary on the history of

Superman, kind of a companion to the film, which chronicles the origins of the character and how he's survived through cultural change in different incarnations, and the Donner movie obviously is very much a part of it. So I was watching parts of the first movie again for the eighty millionth time, in relation to this documentary, and it really is [creative consultant Tom] Mankiewicz and Donner, in terms of the writing... So much of it is in the character moments; the Clark moments, especially the interview Lois does with him on the roof. Mike, Dan and myself never in our minds felt that we could ever do anything like Richard Donner's *Superman* – it's such a classic, you can't really do it better. You can do it a little more modern, or you can do it newer, but if it's classic you can't really do it better. So our first order of business was not to make a remake, because there was so much in that movie that was classic to us; and secondly not to beat ourselves up in the sense that you just do the best you can, in terms of casting and the scenes, and then in the script.

But you also got to kind of revisit the origin story in a unique way.

We call it the inversion of sequences – you've got the classic sequences and you kind of expect how they're going to go, but because we have Superman returning to a changed world, you get to approach it from another angle, where everything's different in terms of the characters. So a meeting on the rooftop between Lois and Superman is no longer a seductive date, it's a painful meeting with an ex-boyfriend who has returned a little too late – I mean, she has a child now. That was me trying to create an obstacle stronger than kryptonite and one that's harder to navigate through, and therein lies the emotional core.

It's something that not only humanizes Superman, it also helps the audience to relate to him.

That's where we took the inspiration from the Richard Donner film – not just how Christopher Reeve made the character [human], but also how the kind of epic storytelling had humanized Clark, watching him progress through the good movies and not-so-good movies – it made the humanization of *all* comic book films possible.

Did you feel that a lot of the origin story, unlike say with Spider-Man or the X-Men, was so well known that re-telling it was kind of redundant?

Maybe. There's some kind of primal piece of information. Every once in a while when people bring kids to the set, or elderly relatives, or people out of the mainstream, you ask them who Superman is and they may not know the specifics – the X-ray vision, the heat vision, the Kryptonian heritage or the details of that – but they will know that he flies, they'll know that he is vulnerable to kryptonite, and they'll have an image in their heads.

So not only do you have a great movie to follow, you also have that legacy. What on earth made you want to take it on?

I've been a fan of Superman since I was a kid – since the George Reeves television show. Having said that, Dan, Mike and myself wouldn't have been prepared to take on something without having had the experience on *X-Men 2* and myself on the two *X-Men* films – I've spent about six years of my life addressing a comic book universe with a fiercely rabid fan base, so there was a kind of preparation that enables you to jump into something like this. And yet when you're casting or developing a costume, it's still intimidating. Even cutting the picture together... Working on the documentary, actually, was the most intimidating aspect because you really saw there was a seventy-year-old legacy. And he's suffered through incarnations that have sparked questions like, 'Is he relevant today? He's such a goody-goody,' and I'm like, 'Hell yeah! Now more than ever.'

He even survived his greatest threat – the latter day graphic novels where every comic book character suddenly needed depth and conflict and angst. In a way, *Superman Returns* finally brings out this conflicted character without necessarily having to go oppressively dark.

That's what I call our modern conflict. Anyone, whether they're wealthy, powerful, handsome, athletic; no matter how successful or virtuous someone may be, all it takes is feelings for another person to bring you down beneath human size, and that is something everyone can relate to.

Let's talk about the actual shooting. Coming off the X-Men movies, the action sequences must have been almost second nature, but what was it like for a first-timer like Brandon Routh?

It took a lot of training and preparing. When you're on fly rigs, there's a lot of pain tolerance, so we had him do a lot of pre-training on the rigs and the wires. A lot of it is 'green screen' and a lot is CGI, but there's still a lot of physical stuff. Plus we also did certain tests for the physics of the thing – what's difficult for Superman, what's effortless, what's painful. With each [physical feat] there's a different kind of reaction required, and there's constant day-to-day discussion and thought. And that's why it's great to have Dan and Mike through the entire process of shooting the film as well, so I've got somebody else to talk to about it besides Brandon and myself! We did tests with Brandon where we put him in a swimming pool, he's a really good swimmer, so he would kick off from one side of the pool and hit the other side of the pool to kind of learn how the body takes impact and stress while in flight, which is a key thing – not only for Brandon to understand, but also for the animators where they're doing sequences where he's rendered in CGI.

Back in 1978 they took great pains to tell us 'You'll believe a man can fly.' Today we take those things for granted, but it's still a hard thing to pull off, isn't it?

Oh, yeah! In *Spider-Man* they had him swinging from building to building in a mask, but here our guy has to fly around with his head exposed, his hair moving, and the cape, which has to interact. These things are challenging, and there are 2,000 people trying to make them work. But yeah, it was an amazing challenge for Richard Donner because you had no rig removal [software] – you had to hide the rigs in shadow. Dick was telling me that in all the tests they did with stunt people you didn't really believe it at all, until Christopher Reeve got into those rigs and sold it with his acting. My favourite moment is when he leaves Lois on the rooftop and he flies backwards. I always thought, 'How the hell did they do that, and hide the rig?' Well, they just lifted him up, he waved, he acted it perfectly, he arched his back, and then they tilted the camera. It's amazing to look at the 'making of' footage.

In the X-Men films you worked a lot with subtext – mutation as a metaphor for puberty, alienation and 'otherness'. What thematic elements did you find in Superman, where what you see is what you get?

What Superman represents is idealism in a physical form. That's the best way I can describe it. You see a scene like the 'coming out' scene in *X-Men 2*, that's what it is – it's very clearly a parallel for tolerance and for younger people who have to face these kinds of situations. With Superman, it's all the virtue and all the pitfalls of idealism. 'I'm here to fight for truth and justice... and all that stuff.' And when you say 'I'm here to fight for truth, justice and the American way,' even Lois Lane in Dick Donner's film says, 'Well, you're gonna end up fighting every politician in Washington.' So people say, 'Is he American?' and I say, 'Damn right!' 'Well, isn't America this or that...?' And I say, 'Well, *idealistically* we're not, and the *idealism* of "freedom for everybody" is pretty great.' And that's what he stands for. That's why I think on this movie I focused more on the relationship aspects, because if you get into the geo-political aspects of Superman – in other words, who does he help, who does he not help? – there are places you can get to that are more challenging. On the other hand, maybe they'll be right for another movie, just go there with Superman and see what happens.

He has certainly been a more political figure in the comics.

In the comic he has attempted to solve social problems, but it's very often fraught with the complexities of social problems, like in *Superman IV: The Quest*

for Peace. During the Second World War he was used as a propaganda mechanism, but he never actually tackled the global problem of the war. He would help at some points – he would take on the Japanese, the Nazis, or Mussolini – but he would never fight them directly, you know, go overseas and clean up, even though he could, because that was for the soldiers. In the end, as much as he's been into it and used for that kind of thing, he's kept out of that big sphere because he's too powerful.

So he thinks globally, but acts locally.

Yeah, and I think that's one of the reasons *Smallville* is successful, because it stays in Smallville. Batman stays in Gotham, and Superman stays in Metropolis.

Which isn't even a real city – and you shot it in Australia!

Donner used New York. I had some guilt about shooting the pastoral plains of Kansas in Tamworth, Australia – then I found out that Richard Donner shot the farm scenes in *Superman* in Alberta, Canada, so I didn't feel guilty about that. The aspect of Metropolis we did differently was we took a mixture of [modern] New York with a nod to the 1930s in terms of the *Daily Planet* and the wardrobe. I mean, there are modern things but the *Daily Planet* and its occupants, Lois Lane and the other characters, feel like they're almost frozen in time, and in that way it's not a period film but it almost could be. It's not set in the world of today, and that's another nice escapist aspect of *Superman Returns* – even though it takes place in a modern world, it puts you in another place.

It's hard trying to set out to make a 'timeless' movie – I'm not sure if Donner managed it by accident or design.

I don't know. I kind of learned that on *The Usual Suspects*, I decided to use these little tricks in confusing the period. For instance, I shot that film in the '90s but I used cars from the '80s, so when you saw the movie in the new millennium, you'd be confused about when it was really made because it wasn't grounded in any specific period. The choice of guns, costumes...

I'm picturing Gabriel Byrne in a kind of '50s pea-coat.

Yeah, exactly! And Stephen Baldwin was wearing this jacket from the '60s, and Redfoot drove up in this big crazy car from the '70s... everybody had an era, and I mixed them up very specifically so the movie would kind of lose you in time. With *Superman Returns*, we applied the same principles – even had the same costume designer, who's with me on every movie – and very specifically

tried to lose you in time. And I think what happened with the Richard Donner movie is, as Tom Mankiewicz tells it, you have three separate kinds of movie in the course of one film: the scenes on Krypton are written like a Roman epic, then it becomes [pastoral artist] Andrew Wyeth on the farm, with a kind of earnestness. And the moment you get to New York...

... you're in a screwball comedy.

Exactly, and the one-liners are flying! So watching it as a kid back in 1978, we're being taken through the history of movies in this one Superman movie, therefore it isn't anchored in any particular time by the nature of its style. So with *Superman Returns* there's a greater consistency in the flow of it. We don't go back to Krypton, so there isn't that kind of breakdown – it's mostly set in Metropolis – but the mixing of it is more in the classic look of Superman combined with the period look of the *Daily Planet* combined with the modern dilemma. That's the attempt at least.

As a fan, you were presumably watching from a distance the development of the previous attempts at making a Superman film: *Batman vs. Superman*, Tim Burton's version...

Not so much from a distance – it was a story of jealousy on my part! I was at a Bob Dylan concert with Kevin Spacey and there were rumours that he was going to be in Tim Burton's Superman. I don't know whether he was going to play Lex, I think it was another villain. And I asked Kevin about it and he said, 'No, it's not confirmed.' I was about to make *X-Men* and I was very jealous of the notion that my friend Kevin was going to go off and make a Superman film! I was like, 'Oh, God! Another guy's doing Superman!' Then it went to Brett Ratner, and then McG, and then suddenly he fell out and Warner Bros. said they were willing to wipe away ten years of development costs and fifty minutes of pre-visualization, art direction, drawings and designs and models and costume tests – it was an extraordinary amount of development work.

Which is a testament to the amount of trust the studio put in you to make a completely fresh start.

Exactly, and it's more than the financial loss, it's the bravery it takes to say, 'We were going in a direction for ten years and by God it was all wrong, and we're willing to go in this direction now.' Whether they're right or wrong, it takes courage to do that. With *Batman vs. Superman*, I felt there was a danger that when you combine major franchises, there's a thrill to it, but if it's not successful, you kill both of them!

And it's many millions of dollars' worth of 'you can't undo it.'

Yeah! But with Superman the nice part is that because it's a core brand, you have certain partners you can work with. Corporate partners.

How do you explain Superman's continuing popularity?

There's something about the image and the icon… you know, it's famous people like Jerry Seinfeld and Shaquille O'Neal who take this icon, born of the Depression, because it represents a kind of idealism - the same thing that makes people proud to be in this country and the ideals of freedom. And I think there's a coolness factor that transcends other icons. Superman is above that. If someone wears a Superman pendant or has a Superman tattoo it means something. It's love of virtue, and also nostalgia, because he's old enough and original enough... it's cool. It's not like having a tattoo of something that's popular in the moment. It's something that existed long before that person was born, and something that's going to exist … long after we're dead. And that's okay to wear, and that's okay to embrace. They're very important, these comic book movies, because they're our modern myths. I never read comics growing up, but I watched *Batman* and *Superman* in prime time, and it was never lost on me that these are the myths of my century, and they're just as important, and they're going to be told just as many times in the next century. And they're classic… I'm an adopted kid, so it has an additional resonance for me just because of that. So I never shame away from it or look at these films as making anything less than *The Usual Suspects* or other films I aspire to make, because these are the kinds of movies I waited around the block to go see. I saw *Superman: The Movie* on opening night with my mother.

And now you've established a continuity of your own for Superman, that's part of the Donner legacy and part of the legacy of the past seventy years, but also your own. At some point have you scratched your chin and thought, 'Hmm, if I was going to do a sequel, I might put that guy in, or follow that storyline...'

Yeah, there are things that come up in this movie where you'll see where we're going, like putting the glowing girl on the lake in *X-Men 2*, you'll see where it's going when you see *X-Men 3*, even though I'm not there...

Like, by the time Superman's kid throws a piano across the room, suddenly all bets are off – how do you make a sequel to *Superman Returns* and not have the kid be part of it?

Absolutely! That's one of the things where of course you say, 'Okay, where's this going to go?' You can't just introduce a concept like that without it going anywhere, you have to address that. And you have to address the Richard White / James Marsden aspect of it all. This movie is simply Superman understanding the reality of the situation. It takes this full movie to understand the reality of, 'Okay, this is what's really up. This is the world I'm now back in. Okay. I got that. What does that mean?'

It's like the amount of time in *X-Men* it takes Wolverine to decide which side he's going to be on.

It is! And in *X-Men* it took a full movie for the audience that wasn't familiar with X-Men to understand this world, and it was all through Wolverine and Rogue's eyes – it was basically their journey to understand the importance of that school, and by the end of it it's the two of them commiserating before Wolverine takes off. So, yeah, I would love to do a sequel, but it takes so much out of you, and it takes two years – but when it's all done you step back and say, 'Oh, well, maybe, okay.'

You can't make these movies fast enough for the audience.

Oh, yeah! They're looking at trailers for *Superman Returns* and asking, 'In the second one...' and you're like, 'It was two years of my life!'

Michael Dougherty

INTERVIEWED BY DAVID HUGHES

An accomplished animator and illustrator, Michael Dougherty co-wrote (with his writing partner Dan Harris) the blockbuster *X2: X-Men United* (2003), which grossed $415 million worldwide. In addition to co-writing *Superman Returns*, Dougherty will be working with Harris and Bryan Singer on a twelve-issue run of *Ultimate X-Men* comic books and the *Superman Returns* comic book prequels. Having adapted the bestselling novel *I, Lucifer* with Harris, Dougherty is set to make his directorial debut with a horror film, *Trick or Treat,* which Singer will produce.

What are your memories of the July 4th weekend trip to Hawaii, when you first discussed *Superman Returns* with Bryan and Dan?

Actually it started before that. July 4th weekend in '04 was where it really took off, but the very first conversation that I had with Bryan was when we were in post-production on *X-Men 2*, so that was almost like April '03. What was going on at the time was that the Superman project at Warner Bros. was up in the air, and there was a big debate as to whether they would do *Batman vs Superman* or the J. J. Abrams script, and I think they were beating around the bush and talking to Bryan about it. He had a certain amount of interest because he's always been a fan of the character. He knew the two concepts they were thinking about, and when we were doing the sound mix on *X-Men 2*, he pulled me aside in a soundproof room and said, 'Wouldn't it be great to do a Superman movie?' And I said, 'Well, yeah, okay, but how can you beat Donner's film?' And he said, 'That's the thing, we wouldn't – we'd make a sequel to Donner's film.' And he pitched me the opening, which is pretty much the opening we have now, and that was it. It was a ten-minute conversation, 'Wouldn't it be neat, what if...' And then we never did anything about it. And then a year later was when we did the Hawaii trip on 4th July, and that's when it became very real.

It's one thing to talk about it, but it's another to actually do it. It's intimidating enough having such an iconic character; it's even more intimidating to know that Donner did such a great job... and then you have the X-Men and Spider-Man films raising the bar for super hero movies. How easy was it to set aside those factors so you could focus on the project?

Not to sound cocky but it was very easy, because I didn't feel like we were trying to outdo any particular film. I think the choice to do a kind of sequel to Donner's film rather than a remake is what gave us that flexibility and that confidence. Not that it would be easier to do a sequel, but we weren't trying to outdo the film Donner made, we were simply trying to create something at least as good and continue his story.

How tempting was it to just tell the origin story, as per *Spider-Man*, *Batman Begins* and the rest?

We felt that most people were familiar with the origin story from seeing it told in Donner's film. Everyone knows who Superman is to different degrees; if you stopped any random person on the street and asked them, they'd be able to tell you, 'Yeah, he's from some planet called Krypton or something that blew up.' If they sat and thought about it, they could tell you his origin. So we had that luxury of not having to really go into it that much, which was liberating.

What were the elements you knew you absolutely had to have in there?

There were certain icons you have to have in a Superman story: the romance with Lois Lane; the elements of dual identity with Clark; Lex Luthor as your villain; and then your other supporting characters: Perry White, Jimmy Olsen... the *Daily Planet* is in essence a character, and the Kent farm.

That could also be stifling, having to include so many elements which might get in the way of the story.

I never felt they were stifling. I felt they were rich characters and rich story elements, so I was happy. I mean, it's easier to have to incorporate those things than to have to come up with things on your own entirely. It was an honour to be able to write a scene that took place in the Daily Planet offices. It was exciting to all of a sudden type words that were going to go in Lois Lane's mouth. So it was never stifling.

Tell me more about the development process. After the July 4th weekend, what happened next?

It was fast and intense because we came back from Hawaii with a rough treatment for the film, or at least for the first act or two. And from there we worked pretty much daily, Dan and I, fleshing out the treatment. We took the rough version we crafted on the plane ride back and then in the next couple of weeks turned it into a fully-fledged treatment around thirty-some pages long, and then when that was ready, showed it to Bryan, revised it, and then he took that treatment and pitched it to the Warner Bros. movie execs, and it was that document that got the movie green-lit. And once they signed off at least on the idea, Dan and I then had to write the script, and we were writing that while an art department was being hired. And suddenly they were fleshing out storyboards and conceptual art based on our treatment, which was really great! It was a really unique way of doing a movie and something that should happen more often, because the art department was upstairs, and every time I had writer's block, I would just wander upstairs and take a look at what the art department was doing, to get some new ideas.

Did the fact that elements were already being created lead to any restrictions in terms of where you could take the story beyond the treatment?

No, there were no restrictions. Everything was still an open book. The story itself always evolves because you're always trying to make it better, and you have to change things for the sake of budget and schedule as you get further into it. But the story that we see in the movie is largely the exact same story that we first crafted on the plane ride back from Hawaii. But as they say, the script is written three times: the first time on the page, the second time while you're actually shooting it, and the third time in the editing room, so there's a constant evolution going on.

Which of the characters evolved the most between your initial ideas and the final film?

I think Kitty Kowalski was the character that evolved the most. Originally she was supposed to be more like Valerie Perrine's character in the Donner film, and she still has a dash of that. But I think Parker Posey brought something all her own to it – almost a dash of insanity. Each time you see her she's wearing some completely ridiculous get-up, and she can also go toe-to-toe with Lex.

In some ways Brandon Routh has to have the biggest shoulders to carry a character with such a legacy. What do you think of him?

Brandon did an amazing job. I think Clark kind of comes naturally to him because, well, he *is* Clark! He's this guy from Iowa who is six foot three and really good looking, but shy and kind of awkward at times... so it was like he *was* Clark Kent.

You're a Superman comic fan, right? What's your earliest memory of Superman?

My first introduction to the character was *Superman: The Movie*. I was four years old when I saw it in a theater. So oddly enough I think everything was then compared to the movie. When I read the comic or watched the animated series, I was almost bothered as a kid that it didn't look like the movie: 'That's not the right music! That's not what the Fortress of Solitude looks like!' So that's why it was really great to craft a film which I felt falls in line with what my memory of that movie was.

In the script for *Superman Returns*, that idea of being part of a legacy is there on the page, with the kid reading the comic book to the footage from Donner's film...

Yeah, it's changed a bit in the film; we have the comic book, but we're not using the Donner footage at the beginning. But even doing things like incorporating that theme into the music, or showing the *Daily Planet* newspaper headlines used in the original film, or referring to events from in the original film, or designing the Fortress of Solitude to look like Donner's movie – those to us were all the things that you do out of respect and tribute to the people who came before you.

In *Superman Returns*, Superman in some ways is more alien than he's ever been, yet he's almost more human too. How did you go about achieving that?

That was the big problem, and it was almost the first idea that we came up with. I think people sometimes accuse him of being boring because he's always the good guy, he never has any issues, so it was a matter of finding his Achilles heel – his emotional kryptonite if you will – because I think audiences are a bit skeptical, and today when they watch a super hero film they want to see a hero who is vulnerable, so that was the first thing we came up with. It wasn't like we sat down and said, 'What if we made a Superman movie and he went up against the biggest, meanest, baddest villain?' It was 'What if he came back and found out the woman he was in love with is seeing somebody else?' That's a problem that anybody can identify with, and it instantly humanizes him and makes him someone that you can relate to. We wanted to create a story that everyone can identify with, and I think we've all been in situations where you try to go home again, or you try to rekindle something with someone you've broken up with. And you find yourself on the outs because you can't – as much as you want to slow down time and prevent that change from happening, it's impossible.

There's a wonderful line in there, "Even you can't stop the world from spinning."

Yeah, that's kind of an inside joke. See, I'm a very cynical person and if I wasn't involved in this movie, I would probably be a little sceptical of it, because when I think about Superman movies I think − although I love them − they're also a little two-dimensional because Superman's always the good guy. People want a certain amount of complexity to their heroes now. They want at least a dash of angst and frustration in their heroes. So what this story allowed us to do was say, okay, we're going to take this character who literally was born in the late 1930s, a character from all of our pasts, and bring him and his colorful outfit, stick him in our modern day world, and watch what happens. Creating a 'return' story allowed us to do that. That's how I think even more cynical people can sit back and enjoy it, because they're watching this character, who still says 'Swell!' and has those old-fashioned traditional values intact, interact in our world, which has lost a lot of that charm.

What Superman comic books have you particularly admired?

There are a few. [Jeph Loeb and Tim Sale's] *Superman For All Seasons* was a huge influence because that one really humanized the character. A good example of that is when you open up the comic, one of the first things you see are what look like black and white photographs of Clark as a baby − you're literally opening up the Kent family photo album and they are just pictures of a normal kid. It's not like he was lifting up couches or trucks or anything − it was him with a puppy, at his birthday party, et cetera, so it was like you were dealing with a person. Then [John Byrne's] *Man of Steel*, which was a great reinvention of the character. That has a fantastic sequence where one of the first displays of his powers is saving this experimental space shuttle. Again, I think that was a comic book that painted the character in a more realistic fashion, because you saw that he got his powers gradually − they didn't manifest overnight. And it really explored who the character was, this guy with a dual identity.

It's important to remember that even though he's an alien, he didn't arrive as a teenager or a twenty-year-old; he grew up on a farm in Kansas.

Yeah, and that's why there's the eternal debate about 'Who is the real guy? Is it Superman or is it Clark Kent?' My position is that in a lot of ways he's a Holy Trinity of characters: he's Clark Kent, the guy raised on a farm; he is Superman/Kal-El, who is the public persona, the celebrity, with the colorful outfits, and a name thrust upon him by the media; and he is also Clark Kent in Metropolis, who is a disguise for that public persona. And if I had to say who the real guy was, I would say it's Clark Kent in Kansas, which is who he was raised as. When he goes home to the Kent Farm, he's dealing with 'Mom', and he can use his powers openly − he doesn't have to hide anything. The other two characters have to hide something: Superman has to hide his real name, and Clark Kent in Metropolis has to wear glasses and hide his powers. Clark Kent in Kansas is, to me, the real guy, because to your parents you're always gonna be a kid. The moment you set foot at home, whatever your accomplishments in the real world, you almost regress back to the age you were when you left. You're dealing with your parents in a way that you remember when you were a teenager, and they're waking you up for breakfast... and you can almost completely be yourself.

What was it like seeing the film for the first time?

It was interesting because the first time I sat down and watched it, I had Brandon Routh sitting next to me, and a few people who were involved in the film but didn't know everything that was going to be happening, because they weren't as hands-on as we were. Brandon, for instance, knew exactly how all of his scenes turned out, but he never got to visit or see many of the scenes involving Kevin Spacey or the other actors, so it was fun to watch it with him because all of that stuff was fresh and brand new to him. I remember watching it and enjoying it, though for some reason my cynical side was saying, 'The people around you aren't liking this,' but when the lights came up at the end, I turned around and people were getting teary-eyed! They were emotionally affected. And it turns out that they genuinely felt the heartstrings get tugged, which totally caught me off guard. It happened to me as well while I was watching it, which also surprised me because I figured that knowing every single twist and turn, I wouldn't be affected at all.

That's harder to pull off with Superman than almost any other super hero, because you know the emotional problems that Spider-Man and Batman are going to have, but Superman is unbreakable and unshakeable, and doesn't seem like he'll have that emotional side to him.

Exactly, and that was one of the things that we set out to do. I remember that when we were doing the treatment and heading into the third act, I said, 'Wow, it would be really fun if we can make a movie that makes grown men cry.' It wasn't necessarily an explicit goal, but we definitely wanted to come up with an emotional ending that would catch people off guard.

It's really the father-son relationship coming full circle that does that, isn't it?

Yeah, and I remember seeing Dick Donner's film with my dad in 1978, and that being a huge father-son experience. And then I went back and watched it again in 2004 and realised that he really did create something about fathers and sons. That first speech Jor-El gives to the baby... I didn't realise at that time how sophisticated that actually is. And that's the best type of film to make, the best type of entertainment to make: something that people can appreciate at every age for different reasons. My grandmother still loves more than anything the black and white George Reeves show, the Superman that she grew up with. For Bryan and I and Dan it was the Donner films, and today's teenagers gravitate towards *Smallville*, which I can appreciate simply because I love the character. There's a Superman for every generation. It's like when you walk into a comic shop, there are many different Superman titles, each with their own continuity, all drawn by different artists, but if you're a true Superman fan you appreciate them all.

Dan Harris

INTERVIEWED BY DAVID HUGHES

Bryan Singer invited Dan Harris and his writing partner Michael Dougherty to co-write the blockbuster *X2: X-Men United* (2003), on the strength of Harris's screenplay *Imaginary Heroes* (which was made into a 2004 film starring Sigourney Weaver and Jeff Daniels, and directed by Harris). In addition to co-writing *Superman Returns*, Harris will be working with Dougherty and Singer on a year's worth of the *Ultimate X-Men* comic books, and the *Superman Returns* prequel comic books. Harris is now set to direct an adaptation of the bestselling novel *I, Lucifer*, which he adapted with Michael Dougherty.

How did you first come to be involved in *Superman Returns*?

It was kind of a group decision. The three of us – Mike [Dougherty, co-screenwriter], Bryan [Singer, director] and myself – were on a trip to Hawaii, over the July 4th week-end. Warner Bros. had approached Bryan to do Superman, and at the same time he was negotiating on *X-Men 3*, and *Logan's Run* was in the pipeline – we had done two drafts of the movie with him for that. So we were at this crossroads and he said, 'Well, what about Superman?' And we were like 'Well...'

What was Bryan's take on Superman?

Bryan had this big idea that he didn't want to make a remake. The other scripts that existed were either remakes of Richard Donner's film *Superman: The Movie*, or had taken it in a completely new direction. He wanted to make something that worked off of Donner's film, respected it, and put it into a kind of 'vague history', and make a movie that moved forward – a sort of return story: to send Superman away for a number of years and then bring him back, so we could deal with the rift that's created when he has to return to a world that has changed or moved on without him. And we thought this was a great way in. So over the course of three days in Hawaii, the three of us went from being scepti-cal about tackling such a huge movie, to getting excited about it, to where we had developed a pretty substantial idea for the making of the movie. And by the end of the trip we had put this into a treatment that was nearly a full movie.

What was the single most intimidating thing about reviving Superman? Was it the legion of fans out there, or the fact that Donner had pretty much done a perfect job?

We respected Dick Donner's movie and we grew up with that being the canon of Superman, and for us the struggle was to make a movie that didn't remake all the great things that he did in his film.

It must have been tempting to do the origin story, like *Spider-Man*, *X-Men*, or *Fantastic Four* – the fashion today is to spend the first hour of the film detailing the origin, and the rest battling a super-villain.

Exactly. That was what was so good about this idea – you could have your cake and eat it too, because you could send him away, and when he comes back, have moments of flashback that give you a taste of the origin story, then you can bring him back and he can be rediscovering things again on screen, so things feel fresh but they also feel like they've got history behind them.

One of the earliest scenes in the shooting script has an actual clip from Richard Donner's film, is that still the case?

I think part of it will happen, but like all movies, the script is a bit longer than the film will end up being. But no matter what, there will be Jor-El footage from the original film. For us it was cool, and it worked well, because we were opening this movie with a big set of luxurious red movie curtains, to reveal a comic book, which opens and then that dissolves into pictures from an old movie, which explodes and turns into a new movie. So it was this historical transition that acknowledged all the previous incarnations of Superman and the different media that he's lived in. That was cool because it gave us a sense that we're part of a legacy here, and [although] we're moving forward from that, we're not trying to rewrite any of that history, or trying to reproduce any previous versions.

What elements of Superman lore, or Superman history, did you know you definitely wanted to include?

There was no studio mandate this time around, which was good, so the treatment was pretty close to what finished up in the movie. But we went in going, 'Well, our character's been gone for five years, so he wants to come back to a world with people that were close to him the last time we saw him, so obviously we'll have Lois Lane, Jimmy Olsen, Perry White and the *Daily Planet*... And it's been five years that Lex Luthor's been in prison, so let's make him a little darker and deeper and more sadistic and out for blood, out for revenge, for being put there. And it's the first movie, so we need to stick with the characters that we know and love, and the villain that we last saw, instead of introducing something foreign this time out...

Having Lex Luthor as the villain also keeps it down to earth, rather than having, say, Doomsday or Brainiac, because Lex is a real guy.

That was absolutely it – he's grounded in realism. And it's been twenty years since there's been a very good Superman movie in theaters, and people need to be eased back into the character, I think. So Lex is familiar, but he's also realistic – he's a human threat. We are using a bit of the myth of Superman in this movie and a bit of the science fiction side of him; bringing him back to Krypton and using Krypton as an important tool, and using this technology of recreating Krypton on Earth as part of the plot device. So Lex just seems appropriate because he was a capitalist on Earth, someone whose devious plans could tie into the science fiction aspect without making it too crazy, or throwing audiences off by having a guy in a rubber suit.

Actually, his plan is not even that different than it was in the Richard Donner movie; he's basically doing a fantastic real estate deal.

Exactly, though there's a tinge of a more evil side to him this time around.

In a way, the story reminds us that Superman is an alien, and yet he also feels more human than he's ever felt on screen, because he has to deal with things that humans have to deal with, like the fact that the ex-girlfriend he still loves has moved on...

That was the biggest challenge, the biggest hurdle and the biggest accomplishment of the film: we know that Superman is pretty much indestructible – only kryptonite can kill him – and that he stands for truth, justice and the American way. He's this stead-fast boy scout kind of guy. So we needed to put him in a situation where it would be a little darker, in the sense that he had some problems that he couldn't necessarily fix right away. We knew we couldn't change his character, because you can't change an icon like that, so the only thing we can do is change his surroundings, and then make it an emotional problem for him. By putting him in a place where his mother is moving on and selling the farm, and Lois Lane has a fiancé and a child with that fiancé, he's put in a really tough place. So we humanise the alien by giving him problems that humans have, that we know he can't solve with his alien skills.

He's the last son of a dead world, he's spent the last five years alone in space, but when he comes back he's more alone than ever.

Exactly. And then this giant plot comes in where Lex Luthor's trying to turn this world into the dead world, the place that he can't live, so it becomes a person's search for identity and home and their place in the universe.

And the closest he comes to finding that is in finding a person.

And the fact that the world *does* need him on a personal level. I mean, when he gets back people were saying the world doesn't need Superman.

It hurts more because Lois just won a Pulitzer Prize for saying just that.

Yes, it's absolutely devastating. And what's interesting is to have it happen right off the bat, the moment he comes back, and then make the rest of the movie have him deal with that, and then one thing after another, and make him realise that this world he's left behind moved on without him and has now left *him* behind.

You said the treatment was 80% of what the movie is right now. What scenes or elements didn't make it into the film?

There are a lot of scenes in the script which have not made it into the movie, because the movie would have been three and a half hours long, and that's what's great about publishing the full script. The return to Krypton is not in the movie, for example. We don't see him there, we only see him when he crashes and comes back, so we're questioning when he comes back, and it's pretty emotional to see him disturbed and we don't know why. There was a scene where Lex Luthor tests the crystal, which we now set in the basement of the Vanderworth mansion where there's a giant train set... originally he tested it in the Arctic, in a glacial area, and he created a kind of giant Fortress of Solitude on the ice, and Lois and Richard flew there with Clark to investigate and take pictures of it, and when no one was looking Clark sunk it and put it underwater. I think the sequence was too big and too weird to exist early on in the script... There were a million versions of the Metropolis disaster at the end of the film, from waves coming in and Superman having to pull a subway train out... crazy things.

You worked very closely with Bryan throughout the shooting, right?

Yeah, we were there from call to wrap every day, all through pre-production and a bit of post. From the day we started writing the movie we were sequestered, attending every budget meeting and production design meeting and pre-visualisation meeting – everything that would possibly impact the story in any way, because any time anything got changed it would filter down to the screenplay and we'd have to make those changes work on paper.

When you were putting this together, how much were you thinking about the modern audience's experience of Superman, be it via comics, the DVDs of the original movies, the TV show *Smallville*...

We were really careful that this movie had to play from eight to eighty – that was the big mantra, to keep things tonally and in storyline in a way that respected that entire demographic, but also make the movie in a way that people don't have to see *Superman: The Movie* or have a huge sense of what was going on beforehand, because we're doing a lot of recapping and flashbacks, and explanation about what the crystals are, what they mean, what Krypton was... There's a scene in the middle of the film where Lois Lane is being quizzed by her fiancé, and we get to go over all the facts about Superman, trying to lay the groundwork not by throwing it out there as exposition, but by weaving it through the whole movie.

It could have been stifling creatively to have to incorporate all these disparate elements, but you seem to have found a clever way to bring them together, and bring the history out.

It works really well in this film because there's no exposition that's straight-up dialogue. A lot of it is filtered in ways like voiceover from Marlon Brando [*Superman: The Movie*'s Jor-El] or flashback to an old movie, or running through cornfields learning to fly for the first time. So it all kind of works itself out over the course of an hour and a half or so, and feels like part of the journey because it's all visual.

Where did the idea of Superman and Lois having a child come from? Which one of you three first dared to suggest, 'And what if Lois had a kid, and it was Superman's kid...?'

I don't remember who said it, but it happened in the first or second conversation, because the first thing we said was, 'When he comes back, Lois should be married.' And we thought, let's take that one step further – let's have Lois married with a child, because that's the kind of family you can't break up. And I think we all turned to each other at the same time, after talking about this movie for about eight hours and went, 'Woah! If Lois has a child, and Superman's been gone for five years, it's *gotta* be Superman's kid, and he's gotta do something extraordinary with his powers.' And Bryan went, 'Yes, but we're gonna hold it back until the very end, and then Superman's going to tell the kid that he's his father, and up until then we don't want to know at all.' So we started working on it as a big reveal.

You sow the seed quite early, so you know people will be wondering...

We knew people would be questioning this the whole time. We've been dealing with fans long enough to know that if you say there's a five-year-old kid out there and Superman's been gone five years, people will begin to speculate. But we did everything we can in the movie to tell people that's not the case. I mean, we've given the kid asthma; he's small for his age... he's nothing like you'd expect Superman's kid to be. It's more like Lois's genes. But it's revealed in a subtle way, and for me, having seen the film, when the reveal happens with the piano, it's extremely powerful – the entire audience just gasps. And Lois Lane is watching, so she knows now for certain. So from that moment on, the movie is all about that relationship. The entire movie becomes about what Lois knows, how does she feel about her son, what is the relationship between her and the kid and Superman when they're in the same scene together... Every scene is layered now with something else because *they* know, and the *audience* knows, but no other characters know.

It has additional resonance because of the relationship between Jor-El and Kal-El, which is brought home when the words Superman says to his son are the same words his father said to him.

It's absolutely the most powerful part of the movie. And what it comes down to is that this movie is about identity, where your home is in the world, and it's also about fathers and sons, about passing the torch from one generation to another, and finding your identity in your father.

Which is a perfect metaphor for Richard Donner passing the torch to Bryan Singer.

Exactly.

SUPERMAN
RETURNS™

The Shooting Script
(Printed here under its production title, 'Red Sun'.)

RED SUN

Screenplay by
Michael Dougherty & Dan Harris

Story by
Bryan Singer & Michael Dougherty & Dan Harris

FINAL PRODUCTION DRAFT – 3RD BLUE REVISIONS – SEPTEMBER 27, 2005
3RD WHITE REVISIONS – AUGUST 23, 2005
2ND TAN REVISIONS – AUGUST 22, 2005
2ND CHERRY REVISIONS – JULY 31, 2005
2ND SALMON REVISIONS – JULY 26, 2005
2ND BUFF REVISIONS – JULY 20, 2005
2ND GOLD REVISIONS – JULY 8, 2005
2ND GREEN REVISIONS – JULY 8, 2005
2ND YELLOW REVISIONS – JULY 4, 2005
2ND PINK REVISIONS – JUNE 30, 2005
2ND BLUE REVISIONS – JUNE 29, 2005
2ND WHITE REVISIONS – JUNE 23, 2005
TAN REVISIONS – JUNE 9, 2005
CHERRY REVISIONS – MAY 26, 2005
SALMON REVISIONS – MAY 20, 2005
BUFF REVISIONS – MAY 15, 2005
GOLD REVISIONS – MAY 13, 2005
GREEN REVISIONS – MAY 9, 2005
YELLOW REVISIONS – MARCH 29, 2005
PINK REVISIONS – MARCH 8, 2005
BLUE REVISIONS – FEBRUARY 23, 2005
FIFTH DRAFT (LOCKED WHITE) – FEBRUARY 11, 2005
FOURTH DRAFT – JANUARY 12, 2005
THIRD DRAFT – DECEMBER 3, 2004
SECOND DRAFT – NOVEMBER 24, 2004
FIRST DRAFT – OCTOBER 14, 2004

1   **RED THEATER CURTAINS,** drawn shut. The kind found in   1
classic movie houses of yesteryear. They slowly open, but
only enough to reveal a small portion of the screen. The
film flickers to life, fading in on an old comic book...

SUPERMAN. A BOY'S HAND reaches into frame and opens it,
revealing drawn comic book panels. The boy reads them
aloud:

> LITTLE BOY (V.O.)
> On a distant planet orbiting a
> red sun, a wise scientist
> predicted his world's imminent
> destruction. Despite overwhelming
> evidence, his pleas to evacuate
> the planet were ignored, leaving
> him and his wife no choice...

He turns the page to a panel of JOR-EL and his wife, LARA.

> LITTLE BOY (V.O.) (CONT'D)
> ...but to place their only son
> into a spaceship and launch it to
> another galaxy, in hopes of
> finding the child a new home. A
> child destined to become Earth's
> greatest protector...

As the boy's voice fades, PUSH IN ON a panel. We once again
hear the panel read aloud -- but this time by the voice of:

> LARA (V.O.)
> But why Earth Jor-El? They're
> primitives. Thousands of years
> behind us.

> JOR-EL (V.O.)
> He will need that advantage. To
> survive.

THE COMIC BOOK PANEL DISSOLVES TO:

2   **INT. KRYPTON - HOUSE OF JOR-EL**   2

Footage from the 1978 version of SUPERMAN. JOR-EL and LARA
place the baby KAL-EL, into a CRYSTAL VESSEL. The footage
is treated, almost black and white, save for the child's
blue, red, and yellow garments. We're in 1.85:1, standard
widescreen format.

> LARA
> He will be odd. Different.

                    JOR-EL
          He will be fast. Virtually
          invulnerable.

                    LARA
          Isolated. Alone.

Jor-El holds up a gleaming WHITE CRYSTAL.

                    JOR-EL
          He will not be alone. He will
          never be alone.

He places it into the ship. And as the hatch closes with
the boy in it, we hear:

                    JOR-EL (V.O.) (CONT'D)
          You will travel far my little Kal-
          el...

Jor-El and Lara stand under a cascading shower of debris as
the craft rises upward and shatters the ceiling.

                    JOR-EL (V.O.) (CONT'D)
          ...but we will never leave you.
          Even in the face of our death,
          the richness of our lives will be
          yours.

3   **EXT. KRYPTON - CONTINUOUS**   3

The ship flies above Kryptonian cities, away from the
planet.

                    JOR-EL (V.O.)
          All that I have learned,
          everything I feel, all of this
          and more I bequeath you, my son.
          You will make my strength your
          own, see my life through your
          eyes, as your life will be seen
          through mine. *The son becomes the
          father. The father... the son.*

As the ship soars into space, KRYPTON'S RED SUN EXPLODES.

Blackness. The familiar notes of John Williams' classic
melody rumble to life. The aspect ratio opens wider to 2.35
-- Cinemascope. MAJESTIC TITLES fill the screen,
interspersed with DAILY PLANET HEADLINES tracing Superman's
history, many written by LOIS LANE:

                "METEOR SHOWER BAFFLES SCIENTISTS"   *
                     "CAPED WONDER STUNS CITY"   *
                 "I SPENT THE NIGHT WITH SUPERMAN"   *
          "SUPERMAN STOPS CRIMINAL MASTERMIND, LEX LUTHOR"   *

"LEX GETS LIFE THANKS TO MAN OF STEEL: SWEARS REVENGE"   *
"ASTRONOMERS DISCOVER KRYPTON INTACT -- SIGNS OF LIFE FOUND"

And then we see the biggest headline of them all:

"SUPERMAN DISAPPEARS"

More headlines follow as the world is besieged with all
manners of trouble: war, famine, crime. Soon, these
headlines push Superman to the back pages. Within a matter
of years, he's all but faded from public consciousness.
Finally, we see one last headline:

"WILL HE EVER RETURN?"

End credits. It is silent. The tapestry of stars stretches
into infinity. But ONE STAR seems to move, gliding past the
others. It abruptly changes course, now heading towards us.

A gently pulsing GREEN LIGHT fills the corner of the
screen.

4   **INT. SPACECRAFT - SAME TIME**   4

The green light grows, illuminating the inside of a SHIP
made of crystalline walls that look as if they've been
grown instead of built. A fine mist covers everything in a
haze. We move through the mist and enter a chamber with A
CRYSTAL POD in the center. Through its shell, we see the
silhouette of A MAN laying inside. Asleep.

A CONSOLE illuminates, and a series of CRYSTALS emerge,
projecting a HOLOGRAPHIC STAR CHART. A gentle ALARM sounds.

INSIDE THE POD, the man stirs. With a brief HISS, it opens.

EYES open. Bright blue. Striking. The man sits up, cloaked
in shadow. He breathes deep, now fully awake, and steps out
of the pod. Light washes over him, revealing a powerful
body and raven black hair. Handsome. Every feature
chiseled.

Finally, the light reveals his face. To some, he is known
as KAL-EL, but to almost everyone in the world, he is
SUPERMAN.

He is dressed completely in white -- a strange, unearthly
material that blends with his ship's environment.

AT THE CONSOLE, Superman touches a crystal and the alarm
stops. Looking at the charts, he seems anxious. Hopeful. He
touches the console, and THE ENTIRE WALL IN FRONT OF HIM
changes from solid and opaque, to completely transparent.

Superman gazes at the heavens when *something* catches his
eye: A MASSIVE DARK SPOT, blocking the stars. He touches
another crystal. The lights inside the ship fade, while
outside...

5   **EXT. DEEP SPACE - SAME TIME**   5

A MASSIVE BEAM OF LIGHT illuminates THE PLANET KRYPTON. It
floats silently in the darkness, without its red sun to
provide heat or light.

6   **INT. SPACECRAFT - SAME TIME**   6

Upon seeing his homeworld, Superman's expression is one of
wonder, hope and fulfillment. Did Krypton somehow survive?

7   **EXT. KRYPTON - SAME TIME**   7

The ship glides over the surface, and the remnants of this
great civilization come into view: cities, monuments, and
canyons. Like his ship, they're all born from the same
crystal technology, but while the ship glows bright, these
structures are dark and quiet.

As the craft flies by, we linger on a cluster of ruins.
Through fine cracks, a faint GREEN GLOW becomes visible.

8   **INT. SPACECRAFT - SAME TIME**   8

Superman scans the terrain, looking for anything that
connects him to this place. But something else is
happening. He seems nauseous. His hand trembles. A single
bead of sweat drips down his brow. He tries to fight it
off.

9   **EXT. KRYPTON**   9

The ship moves through the ruins of a huge DOME, descending
into a VAST CANYON of CRYSTAL MONOLITHS arranged in a
circle.

10   **EXT. KRYPTON - VALLEY OF ELDERS - SAME TIME**   10

The ship moves past one of the structures, and illuminates
a large HIEROGLYPHIC SYMBOL. Similar crests are carved into
surrounding monoliths. The ship moves past them, then
stops.

PULL BACK from the cracked crystal relief, revealing it to
be THE SUPERMAN CREST. The symbol of his Kryptonian
heritage.

11   **INT. SPACECRAFT - SAME TIME**   11

Superman is astonished. Never before has he seen evidence
of his family's fate. Suddenly, the nausea becomes a
crippling pain throughout his body. He leans forward,
bracing himself.

Through the window, he sees a strange SHIMMER around the
crest. It becomes stronger. A FAINT GREEN LIGHT becomes
visible, radiating from cracks in the S. It's the ominous
green glow of KRYPTONITE.

Alarmed, Superman pulls the ship away, toward the edge of a cliff. But instead of finding more land on the other side of the cliff, the surface of the planet abruptly STOPS. There is only a steep drop-off plunging into darkness.

12   **EXT. KRYPTON - SAME TIME**   12

PULL BACK to reveal that this isn't the planet in its entirety, but A HUGE BROKEN SHARD. And on the underside is a layer of Krypton's mantel. It has been irradiated, glowing a pale, sickly green -- KRYPTONITE. More than we have ever seen. GIANT SLABS tumble and whiz by. IT'S AN ASTEROID FIELD entirely composed of the deadly substance -- and his ship is floating right into the middle of it.

13   **INT. SPACECRAFT - SAME TIME**   13

The effect intensifies. Superman gasps in pain. He tries to punch commands into the console, but his hands are trembling. Outside, thousands of pieces of glowing Kryptonite are hurtling towards him. WHAM! THE SHIP IS HIT. Superman falls.

14   **EXT. KRYPTONITE ASTEROID FIELD - SAME TIME**   14

The craft tumbles and spins out of control. Parts shatter and break off. But something strange happens. The crystal immediately GROWS BACK where it was shattered, repaired.

15   **INT. SPACECRAFT - SAME TIME**   15

Superman struggles to his feet. Outside, more kryptonite smashes against the window, cracking it. Crystals work quickly to repair the damages, but it keeps coming. He punches in a series of commands, and weakly utters one word:

                         SUPERMAN
             ...home.

Superman takes one last look at Krypton. Now filled with nothing but danger and despair. Above the console, an image of EARTH appears. As Superman SLUMPS to the ground, he looks back at the sleeping pod and painfully crawls towards it.

16   **EXT. DEEP SPACE - SAME TIME**   16

The ship ROCKETS out of the asteroid field, narrowly avoiding MORE DEBRIS from the shattered planet. It pulls back, faster and faster, past another piece of the planet, and another and another. The ship speeds into the distance, and once again becomes a small glowing speck among the sea of stars.

                                              DISSOLVE TO:

MORE STARS. But instead of the eerie silence of space, we hear the familiar sound of CRICKETS, followed by quiet MUSIC.

17   **EXT. FARM HOUSE - NIGHT**   17

We swoop downward, past a crescent moon, to A FARM HOUSE.

                                                      CUT TO:

A SCRABBLE BOARD, displaying the word ALIEN. A WOMAN'S HAND
adds letters, creating the word ALIENATION.

                    MARTHA (O.S.)
          That's... Seventy four points.

                    BEN (O.S.)
          You're not doing a very good job
          of letting me win.

18   **INT. FARM HOUSE - KITCHEN - NIGHT**   18

BEN HUBBARD and MARTHA KENT, both in their sixties, sit at   *
a table finishing up a game of Scrabble. The kitchen is   *
cozy, filled with old mementos and a photo of Martha with   *
her late husband, JONATHAN. A DOG sleeps nearby. Ben   *
tallies the score. Martha has 409 points, he has 70. Game
over.

                    MARTHA
          I like my kitchen table and I
          want to keep it, Ben. I'll let
          you win when we're playing for a
          new bed.

She stands up and kisses him on the head, passing by a
FURNITURE CATALOG, many pages of which are dog-eared. Ben
looks at the open page, which describes a 'NEW WEATHERED
MAHOGANY KITCHEN TABLE'.

                    MARTHA (CONT'D)
          Plus, explain to me how a table
          can be both weathered and... *new.*

                    BEN
          There's nothing wrong with new.

                    MARTHA
          Nothing wrong with old, either.
          And this table's already
          weathered.

                    BEN
          Okay, okay. What's with the
          attachment to a table anyway?

Her eyes move to the edge of the table, where a child-like
name is CARVED into it: CLARK.

                    MARTHA
          I just like it, Ben. It has
          history...

She trails off and turns to the window. It's as if she
hears something outside.

                    BEN
          Martha?

Ben looks down to see the SCRABBLE PIECES gently vibrating
across the board, accompanied by a growing RUMBLE. Soon,
plates, glasses, and lights start to rattle and shake. The
dog perks up, whining.

                    BEN (CONT'D)
          What in...

The rumbling becomes A DEAFENING ROAR, and through the
window, they see the clouds glowing a brilliant RED. It
grows brighter, until A METEOR STREAKS ACROSS THE NIGHT
SKY. It heads toward the horizon, and with a thunderous
BOOM and blinding flash of light -- CRASHES INTO A DISTANT
FIELD.

Ben immediately heads across the kitchen and grabs a PHONE.
Martha stands in the window, still stunned.

Ben starts to dial, but can't get a signal. He looks up to
see that Martha has her finger on the hook.

                    BEN (CONT'D)
          Martha, what are you doing?

                    MARTHA
          It's alright, Ben.

                    BEN
          But you saw that --

                    MARTHA
          It's just a meteorite. Sometimes   *
          they burn up in the atmosphere
          and sometimes they make it all
          the way down. No need to trouble
          the Sheriff about it.

He looks at her skeptically. She checks her watch.

                    MARTHA (CONT'D)
          Listen, it's late. I had a nice
          dinner, and...

                    BEN
          But--

                    MARTHA
          I'll see you tomorrow night, Ben.
          For Bingo.

>   BEN
>   Martha--
>
>   MARTHA
>   (firm)
>   Tomorrow. Bingo.

She looks at him, stonefaced. He takes another look outside
-- and at her, and realizes what's happening. He sighs and
shakes his head.

>   BEN
>   A meteorite?

She nods.

>   BEN (CONT'D)
>   Martha Kent, I knew you'd be
>   trouble.

19   **EXT. FARM HOUSE - FRONT PORCH - MOMENTS LATER**   19

Martha grins, waving goodbye as Ben pulls out of the
driveway. She watches him drive off, and her smile fades.

20   **EXT. DIRT ROAD - MOMENTS LATER**   20

A weathered pick-up truck speeds down a quiet road.

21   **INT. TRUCK - SAME TIME**   21

Martha anxiously stares out the windshield as she drives.

22   **EXT. CORNFIELD - MOMENTS LATER**   22

The truck pulls up next to a large cornfield. Martha gets
out, gawking at A LONG, CHARRED TRENCH in the middle of the
field, scorching the earth for hundreds of feet.

23   **EXT. CORNFIELD - CRATER - MOMENTS LATER**   23

Martha rushes along the trench, following SHARDS OF CRYSTAL
DEBRIS, until she comes upon A SMOKING CRATER. The smoke
clears, and she sees it:

SUPERMAN'S SHIP, or what's left: a large charred fuselage
surrounded by broken pieces, still glowing from the heat of
re-entry. A similar sight to the day he first arrived.

Horrified, Martha is about to climb into the crater when A   *
HAND grabs her shoulder. She screams and turns just as...

SUPERMAN COLLAPSES INTO HER ARMS. They both fall to the
ground. He stares up at her, weak and injured, uttering one   *
word...

                        SUPERMAN
Mom...

With tears streaming down her face, Martha Kent gently
cradles her son as he slips into unconsciousness.

Then we hear the voice of a very different OLD WOMAN:

                    OLD WOMAN (V.O.)
          In spite of your past, I know
          you're a good man...

24   **EXT. VANDERWORTH MANSION - NIGHT**   24   *

A STATELY MANSION rests on a riverbank with a line of
beautiful cars in the driveway. THUNDER echoes. RAIN pours.

25   **INT. VANDERWORTH MANSION - GERTRUDE'S ROOM - NIGHT**   25   *

Two hands wearing matching WEDDING BANDS hold each other.
The elderly, wrinkled hand belongs to A WOMAN, while the
other hand belongs to an UNSEEN MAN. She coughs. Her voice
is weak:

                    GERTRUDE (O.S.)
          ...and all good men deserve a
          second chance. Like my dear
          Stephen, taken before his time.

A FLASH OF LIGHTNING illuminates a portrait of the
distinguished STEPHEN VANDERWORTH above the fireplace.

                  GERTRUDE (O.S.) (CONT'D)
          From the moment I received your
          first letter, I knew you weren't
          like the rest.

WIDER to reveal we're in the lavish bedroom of GERTRUDE
VANDERWORTH, heir to the Vanderworth shipping dynasty.
She's in bed, hooked up to a dozen medical devices. TWO
TINY DOGS wearing DIAMONDS jump up and down, wanting
attention.

                    GERTRUDE (CONT'D)
          You came from nothing, and worked
          hard to get where you are, even
          if you made a few mistakes along
          the way. Not like those VULTURES
          outside, who never had to work a
          day in their lives.

She spits the line out like vinegar. Outside, A GROUP OF
PEOPLE POUND on the door.

                    RELATIVES (O.S.)
          MOM! GRANDMA! OPEN THE DOOR! YOU
          BASTARD! OPEN THE DOOR!!!

The man gives her a hard pat on the back. Once again, he knows exactly what she needs. He gently strokes her hand and pushes 'LAST WILL AND TESTAMENT' papers towards her.

> GERTRUDE
> You said that if I helped you get
> out of prison, that you'd take
> care of me. And you have. You've
> done so much for me... shown me
> pleasures I never thought were
> possible...

*

ANGLE ON: The man's other hand, fist clenching. Clearly, he put up with a lot in this relationship. She coughs god-knows-what into her hand, then grasps his. He almost pulls away but thinks the better of it. Gertrude takes the papers in a painkiller-induced daze.

> GERTRUDE (CONT'D)
> And that's why you deserve what
> Stephen left for me.
> (beat)
> That's why you deserve
> *everything.*

She starts to sign the will: *Gertrude Vander--* but stops abruptly, coughing. The relatives pound harder on the door. She continues signing, but stops again, coughing and hacking.

> GERTRUDE (CONT'D)
> I love you... *Lex Luthor.*

She smiles, and her heart monitor FLATLINES. SHE SLUMPS OVER. DEAD. The man panics, grabs her hand, 'helping' Gertrude finish her signature. THUNDER rumbles outside.

He snatches the will and KICKS the dogs out of his way. He stands up, majestic underneath the portrait of her dead husband. CLINK! His wedding band drops into her false teeth glass and sinks.

26   **INT. VANDERWORTH ESTATE - HALLWAY - SAME TIME**   26

The door opens. Relatives stand back, aghast, as the man steps into the hall. He solemnly bows his head, almost in regret. Instead, he pulls off A WIG, revealing a slick bald head. LIGHTNING FLASHES, giving us our first good look at:

LEX LUTHOR. Just as suave and sinister as ever. Lex hands the Will to a man, and tosses the wig to a little girl.

> LEX
> You can keep that.
> (to the others)
> The rest is mine.

With a skip in his step, Lex makes his way down the hall and signals to A BEAUTIFUL MAID dusting a large display case containing A MODEL SHIP. The woman smiles, then drops her feather duster and joins him. This is KITTY KOWALSKI.

Lex starts to whistle "SYMPATHY FOR THE DEVIL" as the stunned relatives watch them walk away. The little girl looks down at the wig in her hands and SCREAMS.

                                              CUT TO:

27 .   **INT. KENT HOUSE - CLARK'S ROOM - PRE-DAWN**   27

CLARK KENT'S EYES open, looking up at SMALL STARS glued to the ceiling -- stuck there since he was a kid. THE DOG stares at him, wagging its tail.

                         CLARK
                  Hey boy.

Clark reaches for some clothes and painfully tries to sit up.

PAN ACROSS FAMILY PHOTOS on the wall: taking a bath as a   *
baby, a birthday party, high school graduation. Nothing out   *
of the ordinary. Just the life of an all-American kid.   *

28   **OMITTED**   28   *

29   **EXT. KENT FARM - MOMENTS LATER**   29   *

Clark approaches the cornfield and looks around. The farm has fallen into disrepair -- machinery has rusted, and the field is overgrown. He breathes in the morning air and kneels down, running his fingers through the soil... *remembering.*

30   **FLASHBACK - EXT. KENT FARM - DAY**   30

Clark stands up, but now the field is full of tall ripe corn stalks. We're back in his childhood; Clark is 15 years old. He looks out over the field, surveying the land, then smiles wide and starts to RUN. He picks up speed, SPRINTING through the corn until he's just a blur among the stalks.

Clark yells and LEAPS. He sails over the stalks for a few feet and lands, still sprinting. He leaps again, higher and farther this time, landing twenty feet from where he left the ground. He runs even faster. Up ahead, Clark spots A   *
WATER SPRINKLER in his way. He closes his eyes, and LEAPS   *
AGAIN

-- launching through the air, impossibly high, THEN LANDS.

Beat. Clark looks around. He's not on the ground. He's landed ON TOP OF AN OLD GRAIN BIN. He turns, astonished, realizing he's a half mile from the farm.

                              CLARK
                    Wow.

          Clark gather himself and PUSHES OFF. WHOOSH! In a single
          leap, he soars over the entire field, and using the house
          as a springboard, Clark ROCKETS TOWARDS THE BARN... but
          it's coming up too fast. He covers his face and SMASHES
          through the barn roof.

31   **FLASHBACK - INT. BARN - CONTINUOUS**   31

          Clark falls, bracing for impact. But there is no impact. He
          opens his eyes, totally fine, except he's HOVERING
          horizontally, six inches above the ground. Amazed, Clark
          stands and DROPS AGAIN -- but still doesn't hit the ground.
          Noticing that his glasses fell off, he squints and looks at
          the ground, and his vision CHANGES. Clark suddenly realizes
          he's not looking AT the ground, but THROUGH it.

          X-RAY POV: Beneath the soil-caked floorboards, he sees a   *
          small CELLAR, and inside is a strange egg-shaped object the   *
          size of a crib, covered by a tarp.

32   **FLASHBACK - INT. BARN - CELLAR - MOMENTS LATER**   32   *

          Light pours into the cellar as Clark opens the doors. He   *
          walks downstairs and pulls back the tarp, revealing a   *
          charred CRYSTAL POD -- the ship he arrived in as a baby.

          A STRANGE GLOW emanates from the pod. Drawn to it, Clark
          reaches inside, and removes an object: A WHITE CRYSTAL, the
          same one that Jor-El placed in the ship long ago. It reacts
          to his touch, glowing brighter. The light fills his face.
          He stands up, and as he does...

33   **EXT. KENT FARM - CORNFIELD - PRESENT DAY**   33

          ...we're back in present day. Clark lets the dirt fall from
          his fingers and pats his hands. Dawn breaks, and the GLOW
          OF THE MORNING SUN washes over his face.

          THUD. An old baseball rolls to Clark's feet. He looks down
          to see THE DOG wagging its tail, ready to play. Clark picks
          up the ball, reaches back, and THROWS IT. The dog starts to
          follow, then stops, realizing the ball is sailing through
          the air -- *and not stopping*. The dog looks at Clark,
          confused.

                              CLARK
                    Sorry, boy. I'll get you a new
                    one.

          Clark stares at the horizon, thinking about what to do   *
          next. He looks around -- spotting a pile of TOOLS next to   *
          the barn.   *

33A   **EXT. CRASH SITE - MOMENTS LATER**   33A   *

        Clark walks towards something off-screen. He stops. In   *
        front of him is THE MASSIVE SPACECRAFT, still smoldering.   *
        REVEAL he's holding a shovel.   *

        THUNK! The shovel blade enters the ground.   *

                                                  CUT TO: *

37   **INT. BARN - MOMENTS LATER**   37

        The barn doors open. Clark puts the shovel down, then walks   *
        to the center of the barn. The floor is covered in dust   *
        and leaves. WHOOSH! Clark BLOWS the debris away, revealing   *
        the cellar doors. He pulls them open...   *

37A   **INT. BARN - CELLAR - CONTINUOUS**   37A   *

...and walks down the small staircase. He pulls back the
tarp. His childhood ship is still there, though the crystal
is no longer inside. He gazes at the ship, when something
nearby catches his attention:

STACKS OF DAILY PLANET NEWSPAPERS. Years worth, all
addressed to Martha Kent. Clark sits on the pod and picks
up a recent copy. He scans the front page -- no mention of
him, just typical world news.   *

Using his X-RAY VISION, he quickly scans through stacks of   *
papers. We catch glimpses of the articles. Stories about   *
war, crime, terrorism. He reads through them incredibly
fast, when he suddenly stops. A HEADLINE catches his eye:

<u>'WHY THE WORLD DOESN'T NEED SUPERMAN'</u>

Clark pulls this article from the stack, and his eyes dart
to   *

<u>"...by Lois Lane"</u>

He inhales sharply, and as he reads, we hear the voice of:

                    LOIS LANE (V.O.)
          *For five long years, the world
          has stared into the sky, waiting,
          hoping, and praying for his
          return. We have spent our days
          asking where he went, debated why
          he left, and wondered if he's
          even alive...*

                                              DISSOLVE TO:

MOMENTS LATER - Clark takes the newspaper, dismayed. He
closes the storage area and walks away.

                    LOIS (V.O.)
          *People have always longed for
          gods, messiahs, and saviors to
          swoop down from the sky and
          deliver them from their troubles.
          But in the end, these saviors
          always leave, and we are faced
          with the same troubles that were
          there from the beginning.*

                                              DISSOLVE TO:

38   **EXT. KENT FARM - BARN - MOMENTS LATER**   38

The dog trots across the farm towards the house. It has the   *
baseball in its mouth.   *

                    LOIS (V.O.)
          *So, instead of facing them
          ourselves, we wait for the savior
          to return. But the savior never
          does, and we realize it was
          better had he never come at all.*

39   **INT. KENT HOME - LIVING ROOM - THAT EVENING**   39   *

                    NEWS ANCHOR (ON TV)
          In yet another nighttime siege of
          a Chicago bank, armed robbers
          evaded capture by...

Sitting on the couch, Clark changes the channel. CLICK!   *

                    NEWS ANCHOR 2 (ON TV)
          ...a tornado ripped through a
          town...

                    NEWS ANCHOR 3
          ...a family was held at
          gunpoint...

CLICK! The channel changes to a SEINFELD EPISODE. Click!

                    NEWS ANCHOR 4
          ...a high rise erupted in
          flames...

CLICK! Clark turns the TV off and puts down the remote.   *
He's eating a bowl of cereal. The newspaper with LOIS'S   *
ARTICLE sits folded nearby. Things are weighing heavily on
his mind. THUD. The ball lands at his feet again. THE DOG   *
looks at him, ready to play. Clark smiles and puts the ball   *
on the table.   *

                    MARTHA (O.S.)
          Feeling better?

Martha enters with a laundry basket -- a familiar blue and   *
red bundle inside.

                    CLARK
          Getting there.

                    MARTHA
          You just needed a good night's
          sleep, that's all.

She places the laundry basket on top of the newspaper.   *

                    MARTHA (CONT'D)
          I kept it for you.   *

                    CLARK
          Thanks, mom.

She turns and looks out the window.   *

                    CLARK (CONT'D)
          Don't worry. I buried it this   *
          afternoon.

Martha doesn't respond. She's still staring out the window.   *

                    CLARK (CONT'D)
          Mom?   *

He stands and walks to her, and that's when sees the tears   *
in his mother's eyes. She was just too proud to show it.   *
Clark hugs her tight, comforting her.   *

                    MARTHA   *
          Five years. It was just so long.   *
          If your father was alive, he   *
          never would have let you go. And   *
          then suddenly you're here. I   *
          almost gave up... I thought I'd   *
          never see you again...   *

Beat. They hold each other for a long time. Martha regains   *
her strength, wipes her tears away.   *

                    MARTHA (CONT'D)   *
          Did you find what you were   *
          looking for?

                    CLARK
              (shakes his head)
          I thought -- hoped -- it might
          still be...

                    MARTHA
          Your home?

                    CLARK
          This is my home. That place...
          was a graveyard.
              (beat)
          I'm all that's left.   *

                    MARTHA
          The universe is a big place,
          Clark. You never know who's out
          there. And even if you are the   *
          last -- it doesn't mean you're   *
          alone.   *

She kisses him on the forehead, then moves to a small
mirror and starts putting on earrings. He smiles,
comforted.

                    CLARK   *
          I know.

                    MARTHA
          When are you planning on heading
          to Metropolis?

                    CLARK
          Actually, I was thinking about
          sticking around the farm. It
          wouldn't take much time for me to
          repaint the barn, replant the
          fields...

Martha continues getting herself ready -- puts lipstick on.

                    MARTHA
          What about that girl you used to
          like, Lois Lane? The one you had
          me send all those postcards to? I
          have to admit, I got pretty good
          at signing your name--

Martha sighs. Time for some motherly advice.   *

                    MARTHA (CONT'D)
          You know, since you've been gone,
          the news hasn't been quite what
          it used to be. The world can
          always use more... good
          reporters.

                    CLARK
          All we need is a new belt in the
          combine and she's as good as new.

A long beat. Clark realizes what she's getting at.

                    CLARK (CONT'D)
          Mom, its hard for me to live my
          life... keeping secrets.

She gently takes Clark's hand.

                    MARTHA
          Clark, your father and I wanted a
          child so much, and when you came
          to us...

She smiles and glances out the window.

                         MARTHA (CONT'D)   *
              ...well, much the way you did
              last night...
                   (beat)
              We knew that if anyone found
              out... about you... or the things
              you could do, they might take you
              away... or worse. It was a secret
              your father and I gladly lived
              with our whole lives.

                         CLARK
              I just don't know if I'm that guy
              anymore. I don't even know if I'd
              be welcomed back.

                         MARTHA
              Your father used to say that you
              were put here for a reason. And
              we all know, it wasn't to work on
              a farm.

He sighs. He knows she's right. But before Clark can say a
word, there's a KNOCK at the door.

                         BEN (O.S.)
              Martha?   *

Clark takes the laundry basket off the table, quickly   *
putting it behind the couch -- out of eyesight.   *

                         MARTHA
              In here!

BEN HUBBARD enters with a bouquet of flowers, kisses Martha
on the cheek.

                         MARTHA (CONT'D)
              Ben, you remember my son, Clark.

Clark is speechless. He awkwardly shakes Ben's hand.

                         CLARK
              Mr. Hubbard.

                         BEN
              My, my. The last time I saw you,
              you were packin' up for the big
              city. A lot skinnier too. So, you
              flew in last night?

                              CLARK
                    What?

Clark glances at Martha. *What do I say?* She nods, as if to
say 'it's okay'.

                              CLARK (CONT'D)
                    Yeah.

Still staring at her, Clark notices her dress and earrings.

                              CLARK (CONT'D)
                    Where are you going?

                              MARTHA
                    It's Wednesday night. Bingo
                    night.

                              CLARK
                         (realizing)
                    You two... you're... dating?

An awkward beat. Martha glances at Ben, then gently pulls   *
Clark into the adjoining dining room.   *

                              MARTHA
                    Clark, dear... No one will ever
                    replace your father. But, Ben and
                    I have found something special.
                    Together. And, well, this might
                    all come as a shock...

Clark gives her a look: *just level with me.* Beat.

                              MARTHA (CONT'D)
                    I'm selling the farm. We're
                    moving to Montana.

                              CLARK
                    Montana?

                              MARTHA   *
                    The lakes are great, and we love
                    the fishing.   *

                              CLARK
                    Fishing?!   *

                              MARTHA   *
                    Clark, you've been gone a long   *
                    time...   *
                         (MORE)

                         MARTHA (CONT'D)
              ...and not even you can stop the
              world from spinning.

She kisses him on the forehead.

                         MARTHA (CONT'D)
              We'll talk more tomorrow. Don't
              wait up.

Ben joins her at the door.

                         BEN
              It's good to see you again,
              Clark. Welcome back.

Clark watches them leave, then sits down, staring at the
BASEBALL sitting next to Lois' article. With a heavy sigh,
he SPINS the ball.

40   **EXT. ARCTIC OCEAN - DAY**   40

WIND SHRIEKS. The air is thick with snow and sleet. It's a
raging ARCTIC STORM.

THE BOW OF A SHIP crashes into frame, barrelling through
icy waves. It rumbles by, and A NAME on the hull comes into
view: *THE GERTRUDE*. It's the huge VANDERWORTH YACHT,
complete with a HELICOPTER chained to the top deck. OPERA
MUSIC echoes.

41   **INT. YACHT - BRIDGE - CONTINUOUS**   41

A HUGE WAVE crashes against the window. We're on a sleek,
high-tech BRIDGE. It leans from side to side, rocked by the
waves. A pudgy man named GRANT is using binoculars, staring
out the window, searching for something.

WIDER. Revealing two more men: BRUTUS and STANFORD.
Stanford is at the ship's controls. Brutus, the largest and
meanest of them, is puking into a bucket.   *

Stanford looks down at A SONAR IMAGE of the surrounding   *
ocean, filled with icy land masses. Suddenly, there's a   *
BLIP showing a strange STRUCTURE not far ahead. But just as   *
quickly as it appeared, the blip is gone again.   *

Stanford nods to Grant, who presses an INTERCOM button.   *

                         GRANT (INTO INTERCOM)
              Mr. Luthor?

No answer. All he can hear is the OPERA MUSIC blaring.
Grant looks at the other men. They just shrug.

42   **EXT. YACHT - STAIRWELL - MOMENTS LATER**   42

WIND AND RAIN batter Grant as he exits the bridge and heads
down the stairs, holding onto a railing. He opens a door.

43   **INT. YACHT - VARIOUS CORRIDORS - CONTINUOUS**   43

CAMCORDER POV: FOLLOWING GRANT through the opulent ship,
trying to keep his balance while it rocks back and forth.
THE MUSIC gets louder as he descends into the lower decks.

THE PERSON BEHIND THE CAMERA is covering everything Grant
is doing. Annoyed, Grant swipes at the camera lens.

                              GRANT
                    Get that thing out of my face.

REVEAL: Another "crew member". A skinny, weasel of a man
named RILEY. He checks to make sure the camera is okay, and
continues walking through the ship, videotaping everything.

44   **INT. YACHT - MAIN CABIN - SAME TIME**   44

The MUSIC is coming from inside this room.

Lex hums to the opera and settles into his chair to read a
book. Beside him are more books, half read, with notes and
pages tagged, all on CRYSTALS or MINERALS. His desk is
littered with articles pertaining to SUPERMAN and the
'discovery' of life on Krypton. The cabin is SPRAWLING: High
ceilings, library, grand piano, even a GLASS BOTTOM.

KITTY is at the bar, pouring drinks. The yacht leans to the
side, and the martini glass slides off and shatters. She
grabs another, then hears the CLOMP of footsteps above.

                              KITTY
                    Your "friends" give me the creeps.

                              LEX
                    Prison is a creepy place, Kitty,
                    and one needs to make creepy
                    "friends" in order to survive. On   *
                    the inside, even my talents were
                    worth less than a carton of
                    cigarettes and a sharp piece of
                    metal in my pocket.   *

She sets a martini down. Lex looks at it, annoyed.

                              KITTY
                    What?

                              LEX
                    Is this the reward for the greatest
                    criminal mind of our time? For the
                    man who patiently waited by
                    Gertrude Vanderworth's bedside,
                    feeding her prunes, reading her
                    Dickens...
                         (disgusted)
                    washing her...

He pauses. A memory crosses his mind that can't be vocalized.

                              LEX (CONT'D)
                    ...all so we could live in the kind
                    of opulence a girl like you only
                    reads about in magazines?
                         (MORE)

                    LEX (CONT'D)
          Is this the reward, Kitty?
             (picks up the drink)
                  (MORE)

                         LEX (CONT'D)
              A martini with <u>one</u>, withered,
              olive?

Kitty snatches the martini back.

                         KITTY
              My name is Katherine. And that
              wig makes you look old.

                         LEX
              So does yours. <u>Kitty</u>.

Kitty clutches her hair, embarrassed. She walks back to the
bar, almost knocked off her feet by the rocking of the
ship.

                         KITTY
              So now that we're out in the
              middle of nowhere, away from
              prying eyes, does the oldest
              criminal mind of our time think
              I'm worthy of hearing his plan?

                         LEX
              Small doses for small minds.

Kitty slams another martini down -- FILLED with olives.

                         LEX (CONT'D)
              Thank you, Kitty.

                         KITTY
              So what is it? Clubbing baby   *
              seals or selling ice to Eskimos?   *

                         LEX   *
              Do you know the story of   *
              Prometheus?   *
                   (before she can answer)   *
              Of course you don't. Prometheus   *
              was a god who stole the power of   *
              fire from the other gods and gave   *
              control of it to mortals. In   *
              essence, he gave us technology.   *
              He gave us power.   *

                         KITTY   *
              So, we're stealing fire. In the   *
              Arctic.   *

                         LEX   *
              Actually, sort of. You see,   *
              whoever controls technology   *
              controls the world. The Roman   *
              Empire ruled the world because   *
              they built roads. The British   *
              Empire ruled the world because   *
              they built ships. America built   *
              the atom bomb...   *
                         (MORE)

                    LEX (CONT'D)
     and so on and so forth.
          (beat)
     I just want the same thing
     Prometheus wanted.

                    KITTY
     Sounds great, Lex. But you're not a
     god.

GRANT descends the spiral staircase, dripping wet.

                    GRANT
     We found something.

                    LEX
     Gods are selfish beings who fly
     around in little red capes and
     don't share their power with   *
     mankind.   *
          (beat)
     I don't want to be a god, Kitty. I
     just want to bring fire to the
     people.

Kitty looks at him with a hard stare. She doesn't buy it.

                    LEX (CONT'D)
     And I want my cut.

45   **OMITTED**   45

46   **EXT. ARCTIC LANDSCAPE - LATER**   46

THE YACHT is anchored near an icy shore. Through shrieking
wind and snow, Lex and his crew trudge across the landscape;
STANFORD leads. RILEY has his camcorder, documenting the
journey. KITTY is shivering. Above them, a strange SWIRLING
STORM rages.

Kitty reaches out and touches one of the ice columns. She
suddenly draws his hand away, surprised. The column is
different. Taller, smoother. She takes off her glove and
touches it.

                    KITTY
     This ice is warm.

                    LEX
     It's not ice. It's crystal.

Stanford looks back to see Kitty running his fingers over the
crystal column. She then puts her fingers against her face.
Stanford rolls his eyes -- and turns to Lex.

                    STANFORD
          Why is a guy like you with a girl
          like her?

                    LEX
          Why do beautiful women carry around
          ugly dogs, Stanford? Why do people
          volunteer with the mentally
          challenged? Work in hospitals...

Stanford waits for an answer, but there is none.

                    KITTY
               (from far behind)
          I CAN HEAR YOU!

They climb a crest and stop. Riley lowers his camcorder,   *
awestruck -- staring at an unearthly STRUCTURE on the
horizon. Stanford raises a pair of high tech binoculars.

> STANFORD
> You were right. There's some kind
> of unnatural weather pattern
> keeping it hidden.

> LEX
> I'm always right.

Through streaks of wind and snow, THE STRUCTURE becomes
clearer. It's the size of a cathedral, with crystal
architecture reminiscent of Krypton. It is Superman's
FORTRESS OF SOLITUDE.

47   **EXT. FORTRESS OF SOLITUDE - LATER**   47

They enter underneath towering crystal columns.

> GRANT
> Was this his house?

Lex removes his goggles. He snaps his fingers and Riley
raises his camera.

> LEX
> You might think that. Most would.
> But, no. He lived among us. This
> is more of a monument to a long
> dead and extremely powerful
> civilization. It's where he
> learned who he was, and where he
> came for guidance.

48   **INT. FORTRESS OF SOLITUDE - MOMENTS LATER**   48

They cautiously enter the fortress, gawking. It's composed
of a large central chamber, with smaller adjoining rooms.

> LEX
> (whispers)
> Possibilities... possibilities...

Kitty gazes at A TALL, ADJOINING CHAMBER. Oddly, a large
section of the wall is missing, like something huge grew
there and broke off.

> KITTY
> What's this, a garage?

                    LEX
          You're not so far off, Kitty. The
          leading theory is that he took
          off in a futile attempt to find
          his homeworld.

Stanford stifles a LAUGH. Lex looks at him, cross. Kitty
suspiciously looks at Stanford, then at Lex.

                    LEX (CONT'D)
          If so, even he would have to rely
          on a craft of some kind, and I'll
          bet Gertrude's last dollar that's
          exactly what used to be parked   *
          there.

                    KITTY
          So, did he?

                    LEX
          Did he what?

                    KITTY
          Take off for his homeworld?

                    LEX
             (looking at Stanford)
          Well... we gave him a little
          push.

She sees Lex staring at the vast space, trying to figure
something out. There is no obvious technology here. No
central console for one to "activate".

                    KITTY
          So now what?

Lex looks high above and spots AN OPENING in the ceiling.
He steps directly below it into a faint shaft of light...
thinking. He carefully takes one step forward, then another
and another. He almost seems to be counting to himself.

                    KITTY (CONT'D)
          You act like you've been here
          before.

He rolls his eyes and raises a hand to shush her, then
stops at a PARTICULAR SPOT. Again, there is nothing
remarkable here. Not yet.

VWOOM. Lex is bathed in white light, and the crystals at
his feet start to GROW, stretching towards him. The others
nervously step back, unsure of what's happening. Then we
realize that something is growing out of the ground-- A
CONTROL CONSOLE similar to the one in Superman's ship.

It finally stops, and Lex runs his hands over it like a
concert pianist.

We see that the console's crystals surround a larger   *
crystal-- THE FATHER CRYSTAL -- the same one Jor-El gave   *
his son. It gently pulses.   *

Lex grins at Kitty: *told you I knew what I was doing.* He
lifts up the FATHER CRYSTAL and admires it -- below is an   *
array of openings in the panel. Lex inserts the crystal
into the largest, highest opening -- *a perfect fit.*

SHAFTS OF LIGHT illuminate the entire fortress. WHISPERING
echoes from every direction, and the illumination in the
columns suddenly coagulates into multiple ghostly faces of:

                         JOR-EL   *
               My son...   *

Kitty and the ex-cons step back in fear, staring at the   *
ethereal images of Jor-El.   *

                         KITTY   *
               Who is he?   *

                         JOR-EL   *
               You do not remember me. I am Jor-   *
               El. I am your father.   *

                         LEX   *
               ...and he thinks I'm his son.   *

                         JOR-EL   *
               Embedded in the crystals before you   *
               is the total accumulation of all   *
               literature and scientific fact from   *
               dozens of other worlds spanning the   *
               twenty-eight known galaxies.   *
                    (beat)   *
               There are questions to be asked,   *
               and it is time for you to do so.   *
               Here in this Fortress of Solitude,   *
               we shall try to find the answers   *
               together.   *

                         KITTY   *
               Can he see us?   *

                         LEX   *
               No. He's dead.   *

                         JOR-EL   *
               So, my son. Speak.   *

He eagerly turns his attention back to the hologram.   *

                         LEX   *
               Tell me everything, Father.   *

Lex looks down at the pulsing WHITE CRYSTAL -- and smiles.

                         LEX (CONT'D)
               Starting with crystals.

49   **EXT. SURFACE OF THE OCEAN - DAY**   49

     CAMERA moves over the water, a few hundred feet above the
     surface, following a flying BIRD.

VWOOSH! A SEAPLANE enters frame from below, and the camera   *
FOLLOWS IT towards the majestic skyline of the city of   *
METROPOLIS.   *

EXT. SKIES OVER METROPOLIS - CONTINUOUS (SAME SHOT)   *

The seaplane banks to the left and we continue moving   *
towards the city, into the concrete jungle rife with the   *
echoing sounds of cars and sirens...   *

EXT. METROPOLIS STREETS - CONTINUOUS (SAME SHOT)   *

...towards a YELLOW TAXI that has just stopped in front of   *
a building.   *

> CAB DRIVER (O.S.)   *
> That'll be thirty four fifty,   *
> bud.   *

The shot continues, moving back towards the car's TRUNK. It   *
pops open. The cab driver reaches in and attempts to remove   *
TWO LARGE SUITCASES, but he can't even budge them.   *

> CAB DRIVER (CONT'D)   *
> Whaddya got in these things,   *
> bricks?!   *

Two other hands reach in and effortlessly remove the   *
suitcases. Behind the man, we FOLLOW the two suitcases   *
towards a large plaza entrance. Camera TILTS UP, past the   *
man's back, to reveal...   *

THE DAILY PLANET.   *

51   **INT. DAILY PLANET - ELEVATOR BANK - MOMENTS LATER**   51   *

WE FOLLOW the suitcases over the large Daily Planet emblem   *
on the floor, into: *

THE DAILY PLANET BULLPEN - CONTINUOUS - (SAME SHOT)   *

Reporters, assistants, and copy boys scurry about. Ringing   *
phones. Televisions tuned to news channels.   *

We continue to follow the suitcases through the bullpen,   *
clumsily knocking into one desk after another. People try   *
to avoid them.   *

THE SUITCASES hit a particular desk and a CAMERA falls   *
toward the ground. IN THE BLINK OF AN EYE, the camera is
caught with one hand by:

CLARK KENT. Now wearing glasses and a suit. He
apologetically puts the camera back on the desk, which
belongs to:

                              JIMMY
                    Careful, carefu--

                              CLARK
                    Sorry, Jimmy.

JIMMY OLSEN (early 20s, clean-cut and conservative) looks
up at Clark, beaming.

                              JIMMY
                    Mister Clark!
                         (realizes)
                    I mean, Kent! Mister Kent!

                              CLARK
                    Hi Jimm--

                              JIMMY
                    OH WOW! Oh my God. Welcome back!
                    Hey, come with me! No, wait.
                    Don't move! Stay here!

Jimmy bolts off, leaving Clark standing there, bewildered.
Clark steps a little further into the bullpen and looks
around, as if trying to find *someone* in particular. Two
reporters nearly trip over his suitcases.

                              CLARK
                    Sorry guys.
                         (re: suitcase)
                    Still looking for a place to
                    live. If you know of anything
                    reasonable...

They walk away, annoyed. It's as if Clark isn't even there.
He glances around. Everything is familiar, yet different. A
nostalgic smile creeps across his face.

                              JIMMY
                    Behind you, Mister Kent!

Jimmy hands Clark a plate covered in foil.

                              JIMMY (CONT'D)
                    Here. I made it myself.

Clark peels back the foil...   *

                              CLARK   *
                    It looks...   *

...revealing A CAKE. But the frosting has been smeared by   *
grubby fingers. Slices dug out. Icing letters now read "WE
OM ACK LARK".

                    CLARK (CONT'D)
          ...delicious.

                    JIMMY
          Oh. I guess the other guys got
          hungry.

                    PERRY (O.S.)
          OLSEN!

Jimmy turns to see PERRY WHITE. White-haired, early
sixties, and clearly not happy.

                    PERRY (CONT'D)
          Where are those photos from the
          66th Street birthday clown
          massacre?

                    JIMMY
          Right away, Chief.
               (points to Clark)
          Hey, look who it is!

                    PERRY
          Kent?

                    CLARK
          Hey, Chief. Thanks for giving me
          my job back...

                    PERRY
          Don't thank me. Thank Norm Palmer   *
          for dying!

                    JIMMY
          It was his time...

                    CLARK
          Well I do appreciate it, Ch--

                    PERRY
               (slamming his door)
          And don't call me Chief!

Jimmy reaches for one of Clark's suitcases.

                    JIMMY
          Come on, let's get you set up.

THUD! Jimmy is nearly yanked to the floor by the suitcase's
weight. He has to drag it using both arms. Clark starts to
walk toward the cluster of reporter desks.

                    JIMMY (CONT'D)
          Mister Kent?

Clark turns. Jimmy is motioning toward the *other* end of the room. Confused, Clark follows.

                    JIMMY (CONT'D)
          So wow, you sure are lucky.
          Hitting the open road,
          hitchhiking around the world like
          that. I can't wait to hear all
          about the Peruvian llama rodeo.

                    CLARK
          Llama rodeo?   *

They come to a small desk. Jimmy sets the suitcase down.

                    JIMMY
          Yeah, I kept all those postcards   *
          you sent. Hey, gotta run. I'll
          check on you in a bit, okay?

                    CLARK
          Oh hey, do you know where I can
          find...

But Jimmy is already gone.

                    CLARK (CONT'D)
          ...Lois?

Clark sighs, looks at his desk. It's empty, but next to him is a MASSIVE STACK OF NEWSPAPERS, MAGAZINES, and JUNK -- so much stuff that it's too high for him to see over into the next cubicle.

He lifts up one of the massive suitcases and drops it on his desk. WHAM! The force shakes the wall of papers -- a HEAD rises from behind the wall of papers and GLARES at him. It's a woman in her sixties, cradling a phone. Her name is POLLY. He smiles. She doesn't.

                    CLARK (CONT'D)
          Um... sorry... Hi. I'm Clark
          Kent.

She just gives him a dirty look.

                    POLLY
          Polly. I remember you, but you
          don't remember me. It's okay -- I
          used to be blonde.

But she's still blonde. Polly disappears beneath the
stacks. He glances to his suitcase, about to open it, but
thinks twice. Looking around, he spots a JANITOR'S CLOSET.

52   **INT. DAILY PLANET - JANITOR'S CLOSET**   52

Clark steps inside and shuts the door. He sets one suitcase
on the floor, and the other on a small table. Flips it
open. Inside are dozens of pressed suits and shirts. He
removes books and other items resting on BLUE FABRIC, then
picks up the last item -- A PHOTO of his mother and father,
the Kents -- finally revealing what was underneath:

A LARGE RED S, embossed against a yellow diamond. The
SUPERMAN UNIFORM, cleaned and neatly folded by his mother.
He gently touches the symbol, now just a reminder of his
shattered home. Discouraged, Clark shuts the suitcase and
cleverly hides it behind a storage cabinet.

                    JIMMY (O.S.)
              Hey, look -- it's Lois!

Clark's eyes widen. She's here. He takes a deep breath.
Composes himself. Beat. He walks back into the office.

53   **INT. DAILY PLANET - BULLPEN - CONTINUOUS**   53

Clark walks briskly into the bullpen, but Lois is still
nowhere to be seen. Confused, he notices Jimmy and GIL are
watching something on a TV screen.

                    JIMMY
              See -- right there, in front of
              the guy from the Post.

ON THE TV is A LIVE VIDEO FEED of a press conference taking
place on-board a Boeing 777 in mid-flight. P.R. SPOKESWOMAN   *
BOBBIE-FAYE is at the front of the plane.

                    BOBBIE-FAYE (ON TV)
              ...in the past, the space shuttle
              needed twelve million pounds of
              thrust just in its initial launch
              phase. By piggy-backing The
              Explorer on this Boeing 777--

A HAND shoots up, nearly blocking the screen.

                    BOBBIE-FAYE (CONT'D)
              Yes?

A WOMAN stands up. A little more mature than the last time
we saw her, but just as beautiful and spunky as ever. Clark
stares at her, transfixed:

                    LOIS (ON TV)
          Lois Lane, Daily Planet. Piggy-
          backing -- is that *official*
          terminology?

                    BOBBIE-FAYE (ON TV)
               (annoyed)
          Yes, Miss Lane. It is.

                    LOIS (ON TV)
               (rapid-fire)
          You stated that this shuttle will
          usher in a new era of travel,
          enabling the average person to
          afford transcontinental flights
          via outer space -- but can you
          tell us the exact price an
          "average person" will be expected
          to pay?

                    BOBBIE-FAYE (ON TV)
          I think you'll find that answer   *
          in your press packet, Miss Lane.   *
          Feel free to take your time   *
          looking for it.   *

Jimmy smiles proudly.

                    CLARK
          Jimmy, what is this?

                    JIMMY
          It's the first dual-craft launch
          of a privately funded orbital
          shuttle that uses on-board SRBs
          instead of external fuel tanks.
               (off Clark's look)
          They're going to launch it off
          the back of a jet.

                    CLARK
          Sounds dangerous.

                    GIL
          Olsen, I can't hear her. Turn it
          up!

Jimmy grabs the remote and tries to turn it up, but
accidentally changes the channel to a live BASEBALL GAME.

                    JIMMY
          Sorry, sorry!

As he tries to switch it back, Clark spots LOIS' DESK. He
wanders over. Jimmy notices.

54   **INT. DAILY PLANET - BULLPEN - LOIS' DESK - CONTINUOUS**   54

Her desk is cluttered with books, files, and nicotine
patches. On top of the mess, Clark finds AN INVITATION:

> LOIS LANE, AS A RECIPIENT OF THIS YEAR'S PULITZER PRIZE
> YOU ARE FORMALLY INVITED TO THE AWARD CEREMONY...

Clark beams with happiness for her. She's finally getting
one. He looks up to notice some framed photos: Lois with
her parents; her sister; Lois with a HANDSOME YOUNG MAN;
Lois with a LITTLE BOY; Lois with the handsome young man
AND the little boy. Clark pauses. *Who are they?*

Then Clark notices something on the walls: a child's crayon
drawings. All addressed "To Mom". Confused, he grabs the
photo, looking closer at Lois and these two strangers.

> JIMMY
> He looks a lot older now. Kids
> grow up so fast.

Jimmy appears over Clark's shoulder.

> JIMMY (CONT'D)
> He's even starting to look like
> his mother. Already takes after
> her too, especially when it comes
> to getting into trouble.

> CLARK
> His mother?

Beat. Jimmy sees Clark's confused look, and realizes...

> JIMMY
> Oh gee. Oh no. You've been gone.
> (beat)
> Fearless reporter Lois Lane is a
> mommy.

Every muscle in Clark's body stiffens. He CRACKS THE FRAME.

> CLARK
> Sorry.

> JIMMY
> Don't worry, she has plenty. But
> I'm surprised she never told you.

> CLARK
> I haven't really been reachable.
> Wait. She's married?

                    JIMMY
          Yup. Well, no. Not really. More
          like a prolonged engagement. But
          don't ask Miss Lane when they're
          tying the knot.
                    (whispers)
          She hates that question.

Clark glances back at the TV.   *

                    LOIS (ON TV)   *
          If this launch is as pivotal as
          you claim, why is it only being
          covered by one news network?

Clark sets the photo down, obviously bothered.

                    JIMMY
          You alright? You look like you
          could use a drink.

                    CLARK
          It's almost noon, Jimmy.

                    JIMMY
          You're right.
                    (beat)
          Almost lunch hour. We better
          hurry.

                                                    CUT TO:

THE SPACE SHUTTLE, Roaring through a bright blue sky,
attached to the back of a BOEING 777 JET.

                    BOBBIE-FAYE (V.O.)
          Now, when we hit forty-thousand
          feet, the shuttle will detach,
          ascend, and then fire the first
          of two propellent systems: the
          liquid fuel boosters.

The shuttle does exactly as described, but the movement and
detail seem odd. Fuzzy. Almost like a bad visual effect.

A WOMAN suddenly steps in front the image, and we PULL BACK
to reveal that we're actually in:

55   INT. JET - PRESS CABIN - SAME TIME   55

...and this is just AN ANIMATED VERSION OF THE JET, shown
on a large screen behind Shuttle Representative, Bobbie-   *
Faye. The demonstration continues as she excitedly
explains:

>   BOBBIE-FAYE
>   Then, when the shuttle reaches
>   the stratosphere, the insertion
>   boosters will fire, sending the
>   craft into orbit...

ANGLE ON: Lois, staring out the window in a daze, almost as   *
if she's remembering something from long ago. She suddenly   *
snaps out of it and whispers to a reporter next to her: *

>   LOIS
>   (whispers)
>   I'm sorry, did she just say   *
>   'insertion boosters'?   *

>   BOBBIE-FAYE
>   (overhearing her)   *
>   Yes, Miss Lane. I did.

>   LOIS
>   Right. Of course.

Lois hides a smile, then sits back and looks out the window   *
again. PULL BACK from Lois' window, finally revealing...   *

56 **EXT. SKY - SAME TIME**   56

>   ...THE REAL JET roaring through the clouds, and THE SLEEK
>   SHUTTLE perched on top. TWO F-35 FIGHTER JETS follow.

57 **INT. METROPOLIS BAR, ACE O'CLUBS - LATER**   57

Clark and Jimmy step into a spacious mid-town bar. It's
empty, except for a Japanese business man passed out on a
stool and BO THE BARTENDER reading the paper. They sit.

>   CLARK
>   Just water, please. Flat.

Jimmy gives him a strange look. So does the bartender. He
knows heartache when he sees it.

>   BO
>   You sure?

Clark nods. While Bo pours, Clark notices the TV. It's
tuned to the shuttle launch.

>   CLARK
>   Actually... make that a beer.
>   Please.

>   BO
>   Anything else?

>   CLARK
>   (looks at the TV)
>   Yeah. Isn't there a game on?

Bo grabs a remote, changes the channel to the BASEBALL
GAME.

>   CLARK (CONT'D)
>   Thanks.

>   BO
>   No problem.
>   (then)
>   The usual, Jimmy?

Jimmy eagerly nods and Bo puts down a beer AND a shot of   *
whiskey.

58   **INT. VANDERWORTH MANSION - HALLWAY - AFTERNOON**   58

ONE OF GERTRUDE'S DOGS is curled in a corner, sleeping --
stripped of its diamonds and gaunt. It suddenly perks up,
hearing something.

ANGLE ON: THE FRONT DOORS. AN ALARM PANEL beeps off. Locks
and deadbolts click. The dog growls. THE DOORS SWING OPEN.
Lex marches through the hall, flanked by Kitty and his men.
She's adorned with a huge fur coat and layers of jewelry.

>   KITTY
>   Ack. This place is so tacky. Lex,
>   why are we back here?

>   LEX
>   Kitty, while you were doing your
>   nails, I was unlocking the
>   secrets of one of the most
>   advanced civilizations in the
>   universe.

Kitty spots one of Gertrude's dogs, chewing on a small
bone.

>   KITTY
>   Hey, weren't there two of those?

>   LEX
>   (ignoring her)
>   You see, unlike our clunky Earth-
>   bound methods of construction,
>   the technology of Krypton --
>   Superman's homeworld, was based
>   on manipulating the growth of
>   crystals.

>   KITTY
>   Sounds like hocus-pocus to me.

>   LEX
>   Of course. To a primitive mind,
>   any sufficiently advanced
>   technology is indistinguishable
>   from magic.

BOOM. Lex opens a BASEMENT door and descends the staircase.

61   INT. VANDERWORTH ESTATE - BASEMENT - CONTINUOUS   61

                          LEX
                Cities. Vehicles. Weapons. Entire
                continents! All grown.

They reach the bottom of the stairs. We can't see the room,
but the echo indicates that it's large.

                          LEX (CONT'D)
                To think, one could create a new
                world with such a simple, little,
                object.

Lex removes the WHITE CRYSTAL from his pocket -- the same
shining crystal we saw earlier in the fortress.

                          LEX (CONT'D)
                It's like a seed. All it needs is
                water.

                          KITTY
                    (dry)
                Like Sea Monkeys.

                          LEX
                Exactly, Kitty. Like Sea Monkeys.

Lex turns the LIGHTS on, revealing a sprawling MODEL TRAIN
SET dotted with tiny people and cities. Even planes and
jets circle above, suspended by wires. Kitty SQUEALS.

61A   INT. METROPOLIS BAR, ACE O'CLUBS - SAME TIME   61A

BEHIND THE BAR, another bottle gets dropped into the   *
recycling bin, joining seven others.   *

Clark is barely buzzed. Jimmy can hardly hold his head up.   *

                          JIMMY
                Clark's been doing a little soul   *
                searching for a few years. He saw   *
                llamas.   *

                          BO
                Oh yeah? Coming back must be
                tough.

                          CLARK
                Coming back?

                          BO
                To work.

                    CLARK
          Yeah. Well, you know. Things
          change. I mean, of course things
          change, but... sometimes things
          that you never thought *could*
          change. Look at Lois! A woman   *
          like her... I thought she'd never   *
          settle down...

                    JIMMY
          If you ask me -- 'cause she'll
          <u>never</u> say it -- but I think she's
          still in love with you-know-
          who...

Jimmy takes another drink -- Clark turns to him, intrigued.

62   **INT. VANDERWORTH ESTATE - BASEMENT - LATER**   62

CLOSE ON: A SMALL CHURCH on the train set. Kitty's long,
manicured nails reach into frame, positioning small people
on the church steps, creating a small WEDDING PARTY.

                    KITTY
               (mumbling)
          ...I, Lex Luthor... give you...
          Katherine Kowalski...
          everything...

ON THE OTHER SIDE OF THE ROOM

STANFORD is hunched over a workbench, tools in hand,
looking through a large MICROSCOPE.

                    LEX
          Careful... Careful...

MICROSCOPE POV: The blade of a miniature DIAMOND SAW
touches the edge of the WHITE CRYSTAL -- and a miniscule
piece is SHAVED OFF.

Using calipers, Stanford picks up the tiny sliver and walks
towards Lex, showing him the slice. Kitty's not impressed.

                    KITTY
          But it's so small.

                    LEX
          It's not the size that matters.
          It's how you use it.

                    KITTY
          Still using that line?

                    LEX
          Funny.
               (to Riley)
          Are you getting this?

Riley aims his camera at Lex and gives the thumbs up. Lex   *
rolls his eyes and points to Stanford, who is delicately   *
carrying the crystal sliver towards the LAKE in the center   *
of the model train set.   *

Riley turns to tape him just as Stanford's foot CATCHES on   *
a cable on the ground, sending him FLYING towards the train   *
set, arms flailing. He tries desperately to keep the   *
crystal sliver from touching the water, but it's no use.   *
The calipers and the crystal sliver drop into the center of   *
the lake as Stanford falls to the ground.   *

When he stands back up, he looks around -- everyone else is   *
standing on the other side of the room, having backed away   *
from him and the train set. He glances into the lake to see   *
the calipers UNDERWATER -- and immediately panics, racing   *
back to join Lex and the others.   *

                    STANFORD   *
          Sorry, boss.   *

Lex stands silent, annoyed. Waiting... Beat.   *

                    KITTY
          Wow. That's really somethin',
          Lex.

                    LEX
          Wait for it...

Beat. Nothing's happening.

                    LEX (CONT'D)
          Alright. Riley, shut off the
          camera.

                    RILEY
          But I'm getting it!

                    LEX
          I said shut off the damn camera!

Riley turns the camera off, and the train set lights   *
suddenly FLICKER and DIE. So do the lights above. Everyone
freezes.

                    RILEY
          I think I did something wrong.

                    LEX
          No... that wasn't you.

IN THE MODEL LAKE, a REACTION BEGINS: the crystal starts to
GLOW. The water BUBBLES, covered by a thin layer of fog.

63   **INT. VANDERWORTH ESTATE - HALLWAY**   63

The hallway lights DIE.

64   **INT. METROPOLIS BAR, ACE O'CLUBS - SAME TIME**   64

THE POWER DIES. Bo picks up the phone. Dead. He looks at
his CELL PHONE. It's dead too.

>   BO
>   That's weird. Must be a blackout.

Clark lowers his glasses and turns around. He concentrates.

X-RAY POV: outside, cars slow to a stop, some bump into
each other.

>   BO (O.S.) (CONT'D)
>   Want another?

Clark blinks, rubs his eyes, gets his vision back to
normal.

>   CLARK
>   Sure.

65   **EXT. METROPOLIS STREETS - SAME TIME**   65

Skyscrapers and traffic lights flicker off. THE DAILY
PLANET GLOBE stops spinning.

66   **INT. DAILY PLANET - BULLPEN - MOMENTS LATER**   66

The blackout hits. A collective groan echoes.

67   **INT. MISSION CONTROL - SAME TIME**   67

Large screens display the shuttle in mid-flight.

>   SHUTTLE COMMANDER (ON RADIO)
>   Mission Control, booster ignition
>   is at T-Minus one minute and we
>   are prepping to disengage
>   couplings--

THE POWER DIES. The screens flicker off.

68   **INT. SHUTTLE - COCKPIT - SAME TIME**   68

A crew of FOUR ASTRONAUTS are strapped into seats. A
MONITOR displays the countdown until BOOSTER IGNITION: one
minute -- until their power goes out too.

>   SHUTTLE COMMANDER
>   Mission Control? Come in, over.

69   **INT. JET - PRESS CABIN - SAME TIME**   69   *

THE LIGHTS FLICKER AND GO OUT. The engine dies. The plane
DROPS. SUDDENLY, POWER IS RESTORED just as quickly as it
faded. The plane levels. Bobbie Faye's animated
demonstration continues. Lois and the others exchange
nervous glances.

70   **INT. SHUTTLE - COCKPIT - SAME TIME**   70

The astronauts breathe a sigh of relief.

71   **INT. JET - COCKPIT - SAME TIME**   71

The pilots check their readings, baffled but relieved.

72A   **EXT. SKY - SAME TIME**   72A

The shuttle/jet levels off safely, back on course.

73   **INT. METROPOLIS BAR, ACE O'CLUBS - SAME TIME**   73

THE TV turns on. Power is restored. Jimmy nurses a shot   *
through a straw.

                    CLARK
          When you said Lois was still in
          love with you-know-who... who did
          you mean?

Jimmy turns to him and smiles wide, as if he knows who
Clark really is... but then we realize he's maybe just a
bit drunk:

                    JIMMY
          Did you know I haven't had a
          picture published in two months?

                    CLARK
          No, I didn't. Did you mean that
          Lois is still in love with
          Superman?

A long beat. Jimmy stares at Clark, bleary-eyed, confused.

                    JIMMY
               (drunk)
          I don't remember saying that. You
          must be drunk, Clark.

                    CLARK
                 (sober)
            Actually, I've always had a
            pretty high tolerance.

74   **INT. VANDERWORTH ESTATE - BASEMENT - SAME TIME**   74

      Riley's camera turns back on. Power is restored to the
      train set. Everyone looks around, confused, but Lex
      continues staring at the small lake, waiting...

                    KITTY
            That's it?

                    LEX
            Nope. Are you getting this?

      With shaky hands, Riley aims the camera, as the ENTIRE
      TABLE starts to RUMBLE. It begins small, but quickly GROWS
      in intensity. Everyone steps back as CRACKS begin to form
      in the model LANDSCAPE.

      Throughout the train set, model cities and buildings break
      apart. A bridge collapses. Kitty's wedding party is crushed
      by the church steeple. Trains crash. The cracks grow,
      tearing through the landscape. Buildings shatter like
      glass. Overhead lights explode. A PIPE bursts, spraying
      water.

      BOOM! The sound of something smashing into the ground is
      quickly followed by a CRACK in the floor that travels up
      the wall and through the ceiling. Lex watches, amazed.

74A   **INT. MISSION CONTROL - SAME TIME**   74A   *

                    FLIGHT DIRECTOR (INTO RADIO)   *
            Explorer, not sure what just   *
            happened, but it looks like we're   *
            going to have to scrub the   *
            launch.   *

75   **INT. SHUTTLE COCKPIT - SAME TIME**   75   *

                    SHUTTLE COMMANDER   *
            Roger that. Aborting booster   *
            ignition.   *

      Astronaut #2 opens a panel, flips switches.   *

                    ASTRONAUT #2   *
            Sir, boosters are not responding.   *
            We are still counting down for   *
            ignition.   *

                    SHUTTLE COMMANDER   *
            Can we release the couplings?   *

75A   **EXT. SHUTTLE/JET - SAME TIME**   75A   *

One at a time, the couplings FIRE but do not DISENGAGE.   *

75B   **INT. SHUTTLE COCKPIT - SAME TIME**   75B   *

> ASTRONAUT #2   *
> Negative.   *

CLOSE ON: the countdown. The boosters are only seconds from   *
firing. The astronauts are horrified.   *

> SHUTTLE COMMANDER   *
> Mission Control, we have a   *
> malfunction, can you do a remote   *
> override?   *

79   **INT. MISSION CONTROL**   79   *

A technician tries. Shakes his head, concerned.

> FLIGHT DIRECTOR
> Negative, Explorer. Override not
> responding.

80   **EXT. SHUTTLE - SAME TIME**   80

THE BOOSTERS rumble and shake, emitting smoke.

81   **INT. JET - PRESS CABIN - SAME TIME**   81

Bobbie-Faye continues, trying to stay as upbeat and calm as
possible, but her voice is tinged with a hint of anxiety.

> BOBBIE-FAYE
> Now, if you look out the right
> side you'll be able to see the
> shuttle climb into the
> stratosphere. And if you're
> lucky, you may hear the faint pop
> of the sonic boom--

BOOM! The cabin is rattled by a deafening explosion.
Thinking it's the sonic boom, all the reporters applaud.
All but LOIS.

82   **EXT. SHUTTLE - SAME TIME**   82

THE PRIMARY BOOSTERS HAVE FIRED. The blast starts to melt
the jet's tail. BOTH CRAFTS begin to rocket through the
sky.

83   **INT. JET - PRESS CABIN - SAME TIME**   83

Lois and the others feel the jet rattle and lurch forward.
Bobbie-Faye is thrown to the floor. People scream, pinned
to their seats as they're hit by pounding g-forces. THE
ROAR of the boosters and the sound of buckling metal are
deafening.

84   **INT. JET - COCKPIT - SAME TIME**   84

THE AIRSPEED INDICATOR rockets.

> PILOT (INTO RADIO)
> *May day, may day... boosters have*
> *fired and we are not disengaged!*
> *I repeat, we are not disengaged!*

85   **INT. MISSION CONTROL - SAME TIME**   85   *

The staff scrambles. It's mayhem.

87   **INT. DAILY PLANET - BULLPEN - SAME TIME**   87

ONE BY ONE, TVs all around the bullpen are interrupted:

> TV #1
> ...interrupt the regularly
> scheduled program--

> TV #2
> This just in...

> TV #3
> ...the inaugural flight of the   *
> Shuttle Explorer appears to be
> experiencing extremely serious
> technical difficulties...

All across the bullpen, people approach the televisions.   *

87A   **INT. DAILY PLANET - PERRY'S OFFICE - SAME TIME**   87A   *

While looking over a copy of the paper, Perry hears the   *
broadcast. He turns to a television in his office.   *

88   **INT. METROPOLIS BAR, ACE O'CLUBS - SAME TIME**   88

On the TV, the game is suddenly interrupted by a NEWS   *
FLASH. Clark and Jimmy perk to attention.   *

> REPORTER (ON TV)   *
> We're coming to you live from   *
> Cape Canaveral, where it seems   *
> there is a problem with the   *
> inaugural flight of the new   *
> orbital shuttle, Explorer.   *
> Reports are just coming in, but   *
> it appears that the shuttle's   *
> boosters have fired before
> detaching from the jet, veering
> both craft dramatically off
> course and out of control...

PUSH IN ON CLARK: The moment of decision...

JIMMY
Lois is on that plane.

Jimmy turns back to Clark, but only finds a WAD of money.

89   **EXT. METROPOLIS STREET - MOMENTS LATER**   89

People on the street are all walking in the same direction --
- gathering at a store window full of TVs playing the
disaster. Clark walks in the opposite direction, towards AN
ALLEY.

90   **EXT. ALLEY - CONTINUOUS**   90

In the classic tradition, Clark runs toward camera, ripping
open his shirt to reveal -- NOTHING. Just a white t-shirt.   *
Where's his suit?! He panics, but quickly remembers.

91   **EXT. SKIES - SAME TIME**   91

The jet is dragged upward, carried by the momentum of the
shuttle's thrusters, leaving behind A LONG TRAIL OF SMOKE.

92   **INT. JET - PRESS CABIN - SAME TIME**   92

OXYGEN MASKS drop from the ceiling. All of the reporters
are buckled in, but Bobbie Faye crawls on the floor,
struggling toward a seat. The g-forces are making it nearly
impossible.

93   **INT. DAILY PLANET - BULLPEN - SAME TIME**   93

The staff is so engrossed with the TV, that no one notices
Clark enter behind them and step into the janitor's closet.

94   **INT. DAILY PLANET - BROOM CLOSET - MOMENTS LATER**   94

Clark flips open his suitcase, revealing the neatly folded
suit. He stares at it for a moment, almost hesitating.

95   **INT. DAILY PLANET - BULLPEN - MOMENTS LATER**   95

The door opens again, and a familiar figure steps out: RED
BOOTS. Blue suit. Flowing cape.

SUPERMAN.

He stands behind the staff, but everyone is so focused on
the TV that no one notices he's there. Superman catches a
glimpse of his reflection in a window -- he's still wearing
GLASSES. Oops. He yanks them off, tosses them into the
closet, and steps to an open window. VWOOSH! Superman drops
out.

Polly feels a breeze. She turns to find blinds flapping in
the wind. Thinking nothing of it, she turns back to the TV.
A second later, VWOOSH! Superman flies straight up past the
window.

96   **EXT. SKY**   96

The shuttle and jet climb higher into the stratosphere. The
two FIGHTER JETS try to follow but can't keep up.

97   **INT. SHUTTLE - COCKPIT - MOMENTS LATER**   97

The astronauts flip switches and controls, doing everything
possible to detach the shuttle but nothing's working.

                    SHUTTLE COMMANDER
              Entering Mesosphere in sixteen
              seconds...

98   **INT. JET - PRESS CABIN - SAME TIME**   98

Bobbie-Faye tries to stand, but is immediately knocked off
her feet again. Lois unbuckles herself, trying to reach
her.

99   **INT. MISSION CONTROL - SAME TIME**   99

Mission Control hears nothing but static.

                    FLIGHT DIRECTOR
              Explorer, Houston, UHF comm
              check. Do you read?

A NAVIGATIONS OFFICER sees something else on the radar.

                    NAVIGATIONS OFFICER
              Sir!

The flight director looks over the officer's shoulder.

                    FLIGHT DIRECTOR
              What is that?

100   **EXT. STRATOSPHERE - MOMENTS LATER**   100

The fighter jets do their best to follow, but they can't
fly this high. Suddenly, what seems like a THIRD JET
appears behind them. It gets closer, and we realize it's
not a jet-- IT'S SUPERMAN. He rockets past them, heading
for the shuttle.

101   **INT. JET - PRESS CABIN - SAME TIME**   101

Lois reaches Bobbie-Faye and picks her up, grabbing hold of
a seat with one arm, and Bobbie Faye with the other.

102   **EXT. SHUTTLE/JET - SAME TIME**   102

Superman is getting closer to the jet. Almost there...

103   **INT. SHUTTLE COCKPIT - SAME TIME**   103

One astronaut looks at the other, then at the console. The
SECONDARY BOOSTER is counting down: 5-4-3-2--

104   **EXT. SHUTTLE - SAME TIME**   104

SECONDARY BOOSTERS FIRE, blowing off the jet's tail. BOTH
CRAFTS ROCKET FORWARD while Superman is knocked backwards.

106   **EXT. MESOSPHERE - SAME TIME**   106

The shuttle is climbing toward outer space, dragging the
jet with it. The vast curvature of the Earth is visible
below, as is the blackness of outer space above.

Superman tumbles, spins, then re-orients himself. He takes
a breath and ROCKETS BACK TOWARDS THE JET faster than we've
ever seen him fly. Suddenly -- BOOM -- he breaks the sound
barrier -- BOOM -- he does it again, closing in on the jet.

107   **INT. JET - PRESS CABIN - SAME TIME**   107

Bobbie-Faye and Lois buckle themselves in. Lois straps an
oxygen mask on Bobbie, then one on herself. She breathes
deep, trying to stay calm. Outside, she sees the blue sky
fading into BLACK... then stars. Suddenly, SUPERMAN zips
past the window. She does a doubletake. Did she just see
that?

108   **EXT. SHUTTLE/JET - MOMENTS LATER**   108

ANGLE ON: The couplings, still secured.

WHAM! a BOOT SLAMS HARD on the roof of the jet -- then
ANOTHER. SUPERMAN'S HEAD rises into frame. HIS HANDS press
against the belly of the shuttle.

Fighting wind and gravity, Superman uses all of his
strength to PUSH it upward. THE COUPLINGS strain and
finally SNAP, detaching the two crafts. Superman lifts with
all his might, sending the shuttle into the sky and away
from the jet.

109   **EXT. OUTER SPACE - SAME TIME**   109

With a boost from Superman, the shuttle soars into space.

110   **INT. SHUTTLE - COCKPIT - MOMENTS LATER**   110

                         MISSION CONTROL (ON RADIO)
                    Explorer, UHF comm check. Do you
                    read? Over.

                         SHUTTLE COMMANDER
                    We have... lift-off? I mean,
                    we're in orbit. Everything is...
                    okay.

111   **INT. JET - PRESS CABIN - SAME TIME**   111

The passengers experience a brief moment of calm. Pens,
glasses, and more loose items start to float. For a second
we think we're in zero gravity, then the oxygen masks SLAM
against the ceiling, and THE JET BEGINS TO PLUMMET.

112   **EXT. OUTER SPACE - SAME TIME**   112

Superman watches the shuttle in orbit, then turns to see
the jet spiraling downward. He dives after it.

113   **EXT. SKY - SAME TIME**   113

The jet free-falls like a bomb, spinning uncontrollably.
Smoke trails behind it.

Flying as fast as he can, Superman swoops behind the jet
and GRABS ONTO THE EDGE OF THE RIGHT WING. Fighting the
gravity, he pulls at the wing, straining to stop the spin.

He pulls harder but can't slow the jet down. It's spinning
too fast and hard. The wing strains, bends, and finally
BREAKS OFF. Superman tumbles with the debris, then hovers
for a moment, trying to re-orient himself.

The jet continues plummeting, arcing downward into a
nosedive. Superman races after it.

THE LEFT WING breaks off, tumbling behind the jet on a
collision course for Superman -- WHAM! He breaks through it
without stopping, shattering the wing into pieces.

The horizon spins as the jet careens towards the ground.
Superman races alongside the hull, shooting past the
windows toward the nose. Astonished passengers gawk from
inside.

114   **INT. JET - COCKPIT**   114

THE ALTIMETER is at fifteen hundred feet... twelve
hundred...

115   **EXT. SKY - SAME TIME**   115

Superman grabs onto the front of the nose, pushing against
the jet, trying to slow and control its descent.

116   **EXT. BASEBALL STADIUM - SAME TIME**   116

POP! A BATTER hits a fly-ball. It shoots straight up into
the air. Spectators follow it, pointing at the sky, but
their attention is drawn to SUPERMAN AND THE PLUMMETING
JET.

117 **EXT. JET - SAME TIME**   117

Superman pushes against the nose, using every ounce of
strength he has. It finally starts to slow. THEY FALL PAST
THE STADIUM LIGHTS, past the jumbotron screen...

118 **INT. JET - PRESS CABIN - SAME TIME**   118

Lois closes her eyes. Passengers scream.

119 **EXT. BASEBALL STADIUM - SAME TIME**   119

Players scatter to get out of the way.

HIGH ABOVE

Superman looks over his shoulder -- they're directly over
the baseball diamond and still falling fast. He braces
himself and gives the plane one last massive PUSH.

WHAM! Metal groans as A WAVE OF KINETIC ENERGY ripples
through the hull, travelling the length of the jet until it
FINALLY slows to a stop -- only a few feet above the
ground.

120 **INT. JET - SAME TIME**   120

The cabin jolts. People shriek, not sure what just
happened.

121 **EXT. BASEBALL STADIUM - SAME TIME**   121

SUPERMAN hovers over home base, holding the jet straight
up. Strained, he lowers it as slowly and gently as
possible.

122 **INT. JET - SAME TIME**   122

Lois and the passengers brace themselves just as --

123 **EXT. BASEBALL STADIUM - SAME TIME**   123

THUD! The jet hits the ground, kicking up clouds of dirt.
Superman steps back and takes a deep breath. Exhausted.
Spectators and players stare at him in shocked silence.

124 **INT. JET - PRESS CABIN - SAME TIME**   124

Stunned passengers slowly look up from their seats. They
hear the sound of groaning metal as THE DOOR IS RIPPED FROM
ITS HINGES and tossed aside. The yellow rescue slide
inflates, and Superman steps inside.

                         SUPERMAN
                 Is everyone alright?

They nod, dumfounded.

                         SUPERMAN (CONT'D)
                    I suggest you all stay in your
                    seats until medical attention
                    arrives--

He notices LOIS peeking out from behind a seat. She looks
frazzled, but beautiful. Superman starts to walk towards
her. Reporters step aside. She nervously stands, coming
face to face with the Man of Steel for the first time in
years.

                         SUPERMAN (CONT'D)
                    Are you okay?

Lois opens her mouth, and for once, nothing comes out but a
small squeak. Superman smiles, and gently brushes aside
some of her hair, lightly caressing her cheek.

Other reporters watch them together. A few whisper.
Suddenly realizing that everyone is staring, he gathers
himself and addresses the other passengers:

                         SUPERMAN (CONT'D)
                    Well, I hope this little incident
                    hasn't put any of you off flying.
                    Statistically speaking, it's
                    still the safest way to travel.

Lois just silently stares. With that, Superman turns and
walks back up the aisle. He glances back at Lois, then...

125   **EXT. BASEBALL STADIUM - CONTINUOUS**   125

Superman steps to the doorway, gazing out over the
audience. Cameras are all trained on him. A CLOSE-UP of his
face dominates the stadium's jumbotron screen. People are
still too stunned to react, then... THUNDEROUS APPLAUSE.

126   **INT. DAILY PLANET - BULLPEN - SAME TIME**   126

THE DAILY PLANET erupts into cheers.

126A **INT. DAILY PLANET - PERRY'S OFFICE - SAME TIME**   126A

Perry sighs, relieved, then pops an aspirin.   *

127   **INT. MISSION CONTROL - SAME TIME**   127

SUPERMAN'S IMAGE is projected onto the screens. The Mission
Control staff hoots and hollers.

128   **EXT. METROPOLIS STREET - ELECTRONICS STORE - SAME TIME**   128

THREE DOZEN PEOPLE cheer in front of the store. ALL OF THE
TVs show Superman from various angles.

129   **INT. METROPOLIS BAR, ACE O'CLUBS - SAME TIME**   129

Jimmy stares at the TV, wide-eyed and grinning.

130   **EXT. BASEBALL STADIUM - SAME TIME**   130

Superman smiles. Then, VWOOSH! He soars into the sky.

A second later, Lois makes her way to the door and spots
Superman disappearing into the clouds. Beat. She manages a
weak, confused smile, then FAINTS, slips down the
inflatable yellow slide, and lands at the bottom.

131   **INT. VANDERWORTH ESTATE - BASEMENT - MOMENTS LATER**   131

THE MODEL CITIES AND TOWNS are in ruins. Tiny cars and
people lay crushed in the rubble. Almost everything on the
train set has been destroyed, riddled with cracks and
chasms.

SMOKE dissipates to reveal the stunned faces of Lex's crew.
THE ENTIRE ROOM is in shambles. Water drips from broken
pipes. Cracks have spread through the walls and ceiling.
Lex smiles, looking down at something we can't see.

> LEX
> Did you get that?

Riley is trembling, but still holding the video camera.

> RILEY
> Yeah. I got the whole... scary...
> thing.

WIDER to reveal A HUGE CRYSTAL STRUCTURE has grown up
through the train set. It has spread over the landscape,
towering over the destroyed buildings. It's almost
identical to the Fortress of Solitude and Krypton's ruins,
just smaller.

Kitty bends down, looking UNDER the train set. The crystal
structure has grown through the bottom too, with crystal
tendrils piercing the ground below.

> KITTY
> Lex, your little crystal broke
> everything.

Lex looks closer at the devastation, amazed. Intrigued.

> LEX
> So it did.

132   **INT. DAILY PLANET - CONFERENCE ROOM - THAT AFTERNOON**   132

                              PERRY
                    I WANT TO KNOW IT ALL!
                    EVERYTHING! Olsen: I wanna see
                    photos of him bathed in stadium
                    lights! Sports: how will this   *
                    event change baseball? How will
                    they get the plane out of there?
                    Travel: Where did he go? Was he
                    on vacation? If so, where?

    The staff is packed into the room, writing down every word.   *
    A chewed pen hangs from Lois's mouth like a cigarette.
    Clark stares at her, but she hasn't looked up yet.

                              PERRY (CONT'D)   *
                    Fashion: is that a new suit?   *
                    Health: What's he been eating?   *
                    Has he gained weight? Business: *
                    How will this affect the stock   *
                    market? Short term. Long term!   *

    Beat. Perry stops. The staff just sits there, waiting.   *

                              PERRY (CONT'D)   *
                    Well, what are you standing   *
                    around for? GO!   *

    The staff streams into the bullpen.   *

133   **INT. DAILY PLANET - BULLPEN - CONTINUOUS**   133

                              LOIS
                         (whispers)
                    Gil, how many F's are there in
                    catastrophic?

                              PERRY
                         (interrupts)
                    None. And what's the usage?

                              LOIS
                         (reading)
                    This mysterious electromagnetic
                    pulse knocked out portable
                    devices and entire power grids,
                    causing a catastrophic event
                    during the highly touted--

                              PERRY
                         (interrupts)
                    Lois?   *

                              LOIS
                    Yes?   *

                              PERRY
                    In my office.   *
                         (then)
                              (MORE)

>   PERRY (CONT'D)
>   This goes for everybody. The
>   story isn't the blackout, it's
>   Superman!

Perry and Lois step into his office and close the door.

Clark sits at his desk, and smiles at Polly. Her glum
expression doesn't change. After a moment, he turns and
looks at Lois through the glass walls, and concentrates.
Every sound in the office suddenly becomes LOUDER, until
certain noises are filtered out, everything but Lois and
Perry's voices:

                              LOIS (V.O.)
                    The story is the EMP, Chief.
                    Every electronic device on the
                    east coast goes dark--

134   **INT. DAILY PLANET - PERRY'S OFFICE - SAME TIME**   134

                              PERRY
                    Lois, there are three things that
                    sell papers in this world:
                    Tragedies, sex, and Superman. I'm
                    tired of tragedies, and you can't
                    write worth a damn about sex, so
                    that leaves one thing.
                         (points to a photo)
                    HIM.

        Lois sighs, annoyed, when a MAN walks into Perry's office --   *
        RICHARD WHITE, Lois' fiancee. He rushes to her, and just as   *
        they HUG--   *
                                                                       *

135   **INT. DAILY PLANET - BULLPEN - SAME TIME**   135

                              JASON
                    Hi.

        CLARK SNAPS OUT OF IT, and finds a FIVE-YEAR OLD BOY with
        coke-bottle thick glasses standing next to his desk.

                              CLARK
                    Hello.

        WHOOP! The boy takes a hit off an INHALER. Clark realizes
        that this boy is Lois' son, JASON.

                              JASON
                    Who are you?

                              CLARK
                    I'm Clark. Kent. An old friend...
                    of your mom's. From before you
                    were born.

                              JASON
                    Really? She's never mentioned
                    you.

                              CLARK
                    Never?

        The boy shakes his head.

                              LOIS
                    Jason!

        Lois arrives and wraps her arms around Jason.

                              LOIS (CONT'D)
                    I told you to stay in daddy's
                    office.

                         JASON   *
                  Daddy's office is boring.   *

Clark looks up at Lois, suddenly flustered. He stammers,
unsure if he should stand, offer a handshake, or a hug.
She bends down and kisses him on the cheek. He nearly
faints.

                         LOIS   *
                  Clark! Welcome back! I see you've   *
                  already met the munchkin.

                         CLARK
                  Yeah, we were just talk--

                         LOIS
                       (to Jason)
                  Did you take your Vitamins? Eye   *
                  drops? Preventil? Poly-Vi-Flor?   *

Jason nods after each one.   *

                         JASON
                  Yes, mom...

                         LOIS
                  He's a little fragile, but he'll
                  grow up to be big and strong like
                  his dad, won't you?

Jason nods.

                         LOIS (CONT'D)
                       (turning)
                  RICHARD?!

                         CLARK
                  I saw you on TV, in that...
                       (makes a flying motion
                        with his hand)
                  You're okay?

                         LOIS
                  Oh yeah, it was nothing. Hey, can
                  I borrow your stapler?

She reaches past him and grabs the stapler.

                         CLARK
                  Sure. Oh, and congratulations on   *
                  the... Pulitzer. That's   *
                  incredible.   *

                         LOIS
                  Yeah, can you believe it?   *
                       (turns again)
                  RICHARD!
                       (MORE)

                    LOIS (CONT'D)
                (back to Clark)
            So, I wanna hear all about your
            trip! Where'd you go? What'd you
            see? Meet anyone special?

                    CLARK
            Well, there's just so much. Where
            to begin really--

                    RICHARD
            You screamed for me?

This is RICHARD WHITE, Lois' long-time boyfriend. He picks
Jason up into his arms.

                    JASON
            Hi daddy.

                    LOIS
            I've got to run out. Can you book   *
            his flu shot?   *

                    RICHARD   *
            Already done.   *

                    LOIS   *
            Great. And work some family magic   *
            to get your uncle to stop giving
            me a hard time about my article --
            please?

                    RICHARD
            Again?

Lois and Richard kiss. Clark shifts uncomfortably.

                    LOIS
            Again.

Clark gently clears his throat.

                    LOIS (CONT'D)
            Oh! This is Clark. Richard,
            Clark. Clark, Richard.

Clark extends his hand to Richard. They shake.   *

                    CLARK   *
            Clark Kent. Nice to meet you.   *

                    RICHARD   *
            Hi, Richard White.   *

                    LOIS   *
            Richard's an assistant editor
            here who's basically saved our
            international section. He's also
            a pilot, and he likes horror
            movies.
                (to Richard)
            Clark is... well, Clark.   *

                    RICHARD
          Great to finally meet you. I've   *
          heard so much.   *

                    CLARK
               (eyes Lois)
          You have?

                    RICHARD
          Yeah, Jimmy just won't shut up
          about you.

Clark lingers at the sight of Richard, who he suddenly
realizes looks so much like... *him*. Or Superman. Or both.
Lois gives Richard and Jason each a quick kiss.

                    LOIS
          Gotta run.

                    RICHARD
          Where?

                    LOIS
          You heard Perry. Superman's back
          and he thinks I'm the only one
          equipped to... nevermind.   *

                    RICHARD   *
          To what?   *

                    LOIS   *
          It's nothing.   *

                    RICHARD
          So don't listen to him.   *

                    LOIS
          I'm not! I'm going to the power   *
          plant to look into the blackout.
          Seeya!

                    RICHARD
          When will you be home?

But she's already out the door. Richard and Clark both
stare as she leaves. Both obviously sharing feelings for
her.

                    RICHARD (CONT'D)
          No matter how close we are, that
          woman will always be a mystery to
          me.
               (turns to Clark)
          And frankly, she's a little
          pissed. I was out flying when she
          was... in trouble. Well, I'm sure
          I'll be seeing you around the
          office. If you ever need me, I'm
          right over there.

He points to a large office next to Perry's. Richard takes
a glance at Clark's screen.

                          RICHARD (CONT'D)
              What's that you're working on?

                              CLARK
                    Obituaries.

                              RICHARD
                    But those people aren't dead yet.

                              CLARK
                    Yeah, but you know your uncle --
                    um, Mr. White and that Eagle
                    Scout banner he's got over his
                    desk...

          RICHARD (CONT'D)   CLARK
     Always be prepared.   Always be prepared.

                              RICHARD
                    Right.
                         (nudges Jason)
                    C'mon, kid. Say goodbye to Clark.

                              JASON
                    Bye, Clark.

                              CLARK
                    Bye, Jason.

                                             CUT TO:

A NEWSPAPER HEADLINE:

                    THE MAN OF STEEL IS BACK.

137   **EXT. VANDERWORTH MANSION - DRIVEWAY - DAY**   137

     PULL BACK to reveal Lex reading the Daily Planet. Actually,
     he's just GLARING at the giant photo of Superman. It looks
     like he could explode in rage.

     Kitty appears over his shoulder and looks at Superman's
     photo. Her eyes go wide.

                              KITTY
                    Hell-oh.

     We hear a small YIP. Lex and Kitty look down to see   *
     Gertrude's mangy dog staring up at them.   *

     Annoyed, Lex SLAMS the paper shut just as A bullet-ridden   *
     MINIVAN screeches to a stop in front of him.   *

     Grant, Riley, Stanford and Brutus get out of the van,   *
     sweaty and slightly bruised. Lex approaches, tracing a   *
     finger over a dozen bullet holes in its side.   *

                              LEX
                    Run into trouble?

                              GRANT
                    You should see the other guys.

Brutus opens the rear hold, revealing A LONG CRATE. He and Grant carry it toward the dock. Still angry, Lex makes his way into the yacht.   *

138   **INT. YACHT - CORRIDOR - CONTINUOUS**   138

Clearly agitated, Stanford races to catch up with Lex.   *

                    STANFORD
          So, what are we going to do?!

                    LEX
          You're going to modify it
          according to the plans and attach
          it to the stern. I don't care if
          the instructions are in Russian.   *

139   **INT. YACHT - MAIN CABIN - CONTINUOUS**   139 *

                    STANFORD   *
          You know what I mean, Lex. He's   *
          not stupid. How long do you think   *
          it's going to take him to trace   *
          all that stuff back to me-- and   *
          you. He was supposed to die up   *
          there, Lex.   *

Stanford paces. Lex stares at items spread across his desk: A BOOK ABOUT CRYSTAL GROWTH, VARIETIES OF CRYSTALS, A STACK OF NATIONAL GEOGRAPHIC magazines. Lex clenches, obviously stressed.

Suddenly, he hears something -- the WHIMPERING of Gertrude's dog, sniffing the floor.

Infuriated, Lex hurls the newspaper at the animal but misses. It sniffs, then squats and starts to urinate on the paper.

Enraged, Lex snatches a heavy crystal off the desk, ready to hurl it at the dog, when he STOPS. His eyes go wide, staring at something on the urine-soaked NEWSPAPER... an article.

The dog finishes its business. Lex bends down and picks up the wet paper. He smiles, and hands it to Stanford.

                    LEX   *
          Stanford, you worry too much.

Stanford looks at the stained article, intrigued.

          'WORLD'S LARGEST COLLECTION OF METEORITES ON EXHIBIT
             AT METROPOLIS MUSEUM OF NATURAL HISTORY'

Lex walks out of the room.

                    LEX (CONT'D)
          And find that dog a nice home.

141   **INT. DAILY PLANET - ELEVATOR - EVENING**   141

The elevator is packed with passengers, all reading the
Daily Planet with Superman's photo on the front.

CLARK is crammed into a corner, staring at LOIS on the opposite side. Wherever Lois looks, the photo of Superman is staring back. Annoyed, she watches the floors count down. DING! The doors open.   *

142   **INT. DAILY PLANET - LOWER LOBBY - CONTINUOUS**   142 *

Lois steps out of the elevator. Clark finally approaches.   *

                    CLARK
          Uh, Lois?

                    LOIS
          Hey Clark. How's your first week
          back at work?

                    CLARK
          It's okay. Kind of like riding a
          bike, I guess.

                    LOIS
          A bike?

                    CLARK
          Yeah, you know-- nevermind.   *

142 A **EXT. DAILY PLANET - STREET - CONTINUOUS**   142 A *

                    CLARK   *
          But I was thinking... since I've
          gotten back we haven't really had
          a chance to catch up. Would you
          want to--

                    LOIS
               (interrupts)
          Hey, can I ask you something?

                    CLARK
          Sure.

                    LOIS
          Have you ever been in love?

Clark almost starts to answer.

                    LOIS (CONT'D)
          Or at least... have you ever met
          someone and it's almost like you
          were from totally different
          worlds, but you share such a
          strong connection that you knew
          you were destined to be with each
          other? But then he takes off
          without explaining why, or
          without even saying goodbye?
                    (MORE)

                      LOIS (CONT'D)
        (beat)
    Sounds cheesy, I know.

She steps to the corner, tries catching a cab. It's futile.

                      LOIS (CONT'D)
    TAXI!   *

                      CLARK
    Well... maybe saying goodbye was
    so hard because he didn't know
    whether it would be goodbye for a
    little while... or goodbye
    forever.

Lois doesn't seem to be listening.

                      CLARK (CONT'D)
    And maybe he <u>had</u> to go and he
    <u>wanted</u> to say goodbye, but he
    couldn't find the guts to do it,
    because maybe if he saw you, even
    one last time... Well, maybe he
    was afraid that if he even looked
    at you just... *once*... he would
    never be able to... leave.
        (beat)
    Maybe it was too difficult for
    him.

Lois suddenly looks up at him like he hit a nerve.

                      LOIS
    Difficult?
        (her eyes narrow)
    Difficult?! What's so difficult
    about it? Goodbye! It's easy.
    What's so hard about saying
    goodbye?

                      CLARK
    Who are we talking about?

                      LOIS
    Nobody. Forget I said anything.
    TAXI!

She whistles and waves for a cab, while Clark looks around,
awkwardly. He knows exactly who she's talking about.

                      CLARK
    So... do you want to grab a quick
    bite? Catch up? My treat.

                          LOIS
          Oh I'd love to, but Daddy took
          the car and it's my turn to   *
          "cook" the family dinner, which
          means I've got just enough time
          to get back to the 'suburbs' and   *
          order the Chinese food.

                          CLARK
          Suburbs?   *

                          LOIS   *
          Yeah, we have a really nice place   *
          on the river. You should drop in   *
          sometime.   *

                          CLARK   *
          I'd love to.   *

Lois tries one more time to get a cab. Clark notices, and
WHISTLES. The sound is loud and piercing. A small dog
WHIMPERS. A CAB immediately screeches to the corner. Lois
is impressed.

                          LOIS   *
          Wow, thanks.

She climbs in.

                          LOIS (CONT'D)
                    (to the cab driver)
          312 Riverside Drive.

She turns and looks out the open window at Clark.

                          LOIS (CONT'D)
          G'night, Clark.   *

Clark watches the cab drive off. He sighs.

                          CLARK   *
          Goodbye, Lois.

143   **EXT. METROPOLIS STREETS - VARIOUS - MOMENTS LATER**   143

Sidewalks are crammed with people heading home. A breeze
picks up. A strange wind echoes between the buildings.
People look up, trying to find the source of the sound.

A FIGURE appears on the horizon, cruising through the air,
darting between and over the skyscrapers: SUPERMAN.

All over the city, the people of Metropolis see him soaring
overhead: a hot dog vendor, a traffic cop, people at a bus
stop. A mother points him out to her young daughter.

IN THE AIR

Superman looks down at the people and smiles, then makes a sharp right and heads out of Metropolis.

144   **EXT. RIVER - NIGHT**   144

The noise of the city fades as Superman flies along the river. He looks down, gazing at rows of houses on the shore. Spotting one, he slows down.

145   **EXT. SUBURBAN HOUSE - CONTINUOUS**   145

It's a large suburban home nestled near the riverbank. A SEAPLANE floats next to a small dock, which leads to a yard and swingset. Lights are on. Superman quietly descends past the trees, and hovers outside.

Inside, he can hear the first few notes of "Heart & Soul" being played over and over again. He stares for a moment, then focuses.

X-RAY VISION POV: A child's bedroom on the second floor. The parents' bedroom across the hall. Both are messy.

Superman goes in for a closer look...

145A   **INT. LOIS LANE'S HOUSE - KITCHEN**   145A

Lois is setting down boxes of Chinese takeout while Richard fumbles with chop sticks. Jason plays "heart and soul" on a small electronic keyboard.

                    LOIS
          Kung Pao shrimp.

                    JASON
          Mine!

                    LOIS
          Nice try, kiddo. No peanuts, no
          seafood, and definitely no won-
          tons.
               (opens boxes for him)
          Just rice and snowpeas for you.

Jason sneers, goes back to playing on the keyboard.

                    RICHARD
          Why do we get Chinese food if
          he's allergic?

                  LOIS
Because he loves the peas. And I
think we all prefer egg rolls
over macrobiotic shakes.

                  JASON
Macrobiot-ICK.

                  RICHARD
Good point.

Beat. There's an awkward moment of silence. Richard looks
over to see Lois scooping out food for everyone, but giving
herself a small portion. Something is on his mind. Beat.

                  RICHARD (CONT'D)
I've noticed you've been acting a
little different lately...

                  LOIS
Have I?

                  RICHARD
And I promised myself I'd never
ask you about this -- but now
that he's back...
                (beat)
Your article...   *

                  LOIS   *
'Why the world doesn't need   *
Superman?'   *

                  RICHARD   *
No, no -- the other one -- from   *
years ago, before we met.   *

                  LOIS   *
Which article? I wrote dozens   *
about him. I was practically his   *
press agent.   *

                  RICHARD   *
'I Spent the Night With Superman'   *

                  LOIS   *
Richard, come on -- that was just   *
a title for an interview. Plus,   *
it was your uncle Perry's idea.   *

                  RICHARD   *
No, no, no... it's okay, I was...

                  LOIS
Richard, that was a long time
ago.

Clearly you can tell by the trepidation in her voice, it was not long enough. Beat.

> RICHARD
> Were you in love with him?

> LOIS
> He was *Superman*. Everyone was in
> love with him.

> RICHARD
> But were you?

Lois turns -- stares directly at him.

> LOIS
> No.

145B **EXT. LOIS LANE'S HOUSE - SAME TIME**   145B

Superman watches Lois and Richard, having listened to the whole conversation. He sighs, then rises into the sky.

146 **INT. LOIS' HOUSE - KITCHEN - SAME TIME**   146

Lois picks at some food, then suddenly stops and turns to the window, staring into their backyard. Beat.

> RICHARD
> Lois? You okay?

Lois snaps out of it, turns back to the table.

> LOIS
> Yeah. Sorry. Hey, didn't I have
> four won-tons?

She sees Jason stuffing a won-ton into his mouth. She panics.

> LOIS (CONT'D)
> JASON!

Lois and Richard dive, trying to snatch it from his mouth.

147 **EXT. SKIES OVER LOIS' HOUSE - MOMENTS LATER**   147

Obviously bothered, Superman flies STRAIGHT UP, rising above the city. Music swells as we hear the familiar voice   *
of:

> JOR-EL (V.O.)
> *Even though you were raised as a*   *
> *human being, you are not one of*   *
> *them.*   *

VWOOSH! He passes through a cloud layer.   *

                         JOR-EL (V.O.) (CONT'D)
                    They can be a great people Kal-
                    El. They wish to be...

Superman rockets through another cloud layer. He doesn't
cry, but his eyes are welling up -- and it isn't the wind.

                         JOR-EL (V.O.) (CONT'D)
                    They only lack the light to show
                    them the way. For this reason
                    above all, their capacity for
                    good...

VWOOSH! He passes through another cloud bank...

148   **EXT. ABOVE THE EARTH - SUPERMAN'S PERCH - CONTINUOUS**   148

                         JOR-EL (V.O.)
                    I have sent them you... my only
                    son.

Superman settles at the edge of space, hovering. It is
truly majestic. He closes his eyes and bows his head,
almost as if meditating. Then we realize he is actually
LISTENING. WE HEAR WHAT SUPERMAN HEARS: layers of voices,
radio chatter, television signals, thunderstorms,
EVERYTHING. The sounds come quickly, overlapping --
building to a chorus.

He focuses to filter out the more chaotic sounds, then
hears it: A RINGING ALARM. He opens his eyes, and with a
powerful SONIC BOOM, Superman is off...

A149   **OMITTED**   A149

B149   **OMITTED**   B149

149   **EXT. BANK - ROOFTOP - NIGHT**   149

AN ALARM BLARES. THE ROOFTOP DOOR bursts open, revealing
THREE HEAVILY ARMED ROBBERS. They meet A FOURTH ROBBER, THE
GUNMAN, who is in the midst of assembling a large piece of
machinery. A HELICOPTER sits nearby, its blades already
spinning. The men throw the bags of money inside.

                         ROBBER 1
                    Sounds like a lot of them down
                    there.

The Gunman just GRINS and reveals what he's been
assembling: A HUGE TRIPOD-MOUNTED GATLING GUN. He swings it
around, moving it towards the edge of the roof.

CAMERA FOLLOWS THE GUN as it's pointed down towards the
street, revealing:

SIX POLICE CARS positioned in front of the bank.   *

150B   **EXT. STREET - SAME TIME**   150B

         The cops take their places and aim their weapons upward   *
         just as--

         BOOOM! A HAIL OF GUNFIRE RAINS DOWN from the roof, but not
         any ordinary gunfire. They're GLOWING TRACER BULLETS. BOOM!
         BOOM! BOOM! The cops scatter for cover as their cars
         explode.

150C   **EXT. BANK - ROOFTOP - SAME TIME**   150C

         FROM ABOVE, we see the tracer bullets streaming downward,
         tearing apart the police cars in a matter of seconds.

151   **INT. BANK - STAIRWELL - SAME TIME**   151

         TWO BANK SECURITY GUARDS creep slowly out of a hiding spot   *
         behind the stairwell EXIT DOOR. Hearing the sound of   *
         gunfire and explosions outside, the first guard turns to   *
         his partner...   *

                              BANK GUARD #1
                           (nervous)
                       You ready?

         His partner nods. They both raise their guns.

152   **EXT. BANK - ROOFTOP - CONTINUOUS**   152

         THE GUARDS BURST THROUGH THE DOOR AND FIRE. THE GUNMAN is
         hit in the back, but the bullets don't penetrate his flak
         vest.

         HE SWIVELS THE GUN AROUND, aiming it right at the guards.
         BOOM! BOOM! BOOM!

         WE FOLLOW TRACER BULLETS as they blast from the gun and
         tear across the rooftop.

         BULLET POV: closing in on the terrified face of ONE OF THE
         GUARDS. Suddenly, A BLURRY RED STREAK zips PAST THE
         BULLETS. The streak stops, and quickly comes into focus --
         THE SUPERMAN SHIELD.   *

PING! PING! PING! THE TRACERS RICOCHET off of the emblem.

PULL BACK, to reveal SUPERMAN IN HIS CLASSIC HEROIC POSE, hundreds of bullets bouncing off of his body. The other robbers hit the ground, shielding themselves from the ricocheting bullets.

Superman calmly walks towards the gatling gun, deflecting more bullets. Suddenly-- CLICK - CLICK! It's empty.

Panicked, the Gunman pulls out a PISTOL and aims it point-blank at SUPERMAN'S EYE. BOOM! He fires.

CLOSE ON: The bullet. It exits the barrel AND BOUNCES OFF OF HIS EYE, then plops to the ground.

ANGLE ON: the stunned robbers.

ANGLE ON: Superman. He shakes his head.

                                          SMASH CUT TO:

153   **EXT. BANK ROOFTOP - MOMENTS LATER**   153

THE POLICE OFFICERS burst onto the rooftop, guns raised. THE CAPTAIN drops his jaw and lowers his weapon. The two bank guards are smiling at them.

                        BANK GUARD
             What took you guys so long?

WIDER. The helicopter's propeller lazily spins like a mobile toy, revealing EACH ROBBER wrapped up in a different blade.

154   **EXT. METROPOLIS STREET - SAME TIME**   154

A CAR SPEEDS OUT OF CONTROL, tearing through a city street.
Inside, a WOMAN is screaming as loud as she can.

155   **INT. CAR - SAME TIME**   155

She frantically presses the brakes over and over again, but
they don't work.

>   WOMAN (O.S.)
>   SOMEBODY STOP THIS THING!!!

She spins the wheel, narrowly avoiding a business man, but
it launches her onto a sidewalk and straight for A CROWDED
CITY SQUARE.

156   **EXT. METROPOLIS SQUARE - SAME TIME**   156

The car crashes through an empty park bench, but doesn't
slow down. Pigeons fly. She screams louder, closes her
eyes.

People near a booth look up as the car screeches toward
them. They SCREAM and try to get out of the way.

157   **INT. CAR - SAME TIME**   157

The woman covers over her face, still screaming.

THROUGH THE WINDOW, we can tell the car is not only slowing
down, but RISING UPWARD, past the park benches and over a
fountain.

She finally opens her eyes and looks outside. From here, it
looks like the car is HOVERING over the square.

158   **EXT. CAR - SAME TIME**   158

The entire car has been hoisted onto Superman's shoulders.
He holds it over his head for a moment, in a vaguely
familiar heroic pose, then gently lowers the car to the
ground. A crowd swarms. Superman opens the door.

                              SUPERMAN
                    Miss, are you alright?

She steps out. Her hair is frazzled and make-up smeared,
but it is none other than KITTY KOWALSKI. Her eyes travel
up his legs, his body, and finally to his face.

                              KITTY
                         (gasps)
                    My heart!

She falls back. He catches her. A crowd gathers and a young
teenage boy steps forward and points his PHONE at them.
FLASH!

                              SUPERMAN
                    I'm sorry?

Kitty stares up at him, clutching her chest -- then
dramatically poses as another FLASH from the kid's camera-
phone goes off.

                              KITTY
                    Heart palpitation! I have a heart
                    palpitation... And a murmur!
                         (winces)
                    And my back -- I think I ruptured
                    a... a cylinder.

Superman uses his x-ray vision, scans her body.

                              SUPERMAN
                    I don't see anything wro--

                              KITTY
                    Please... take me to a hospital.

She "passes out". Superman looks around. Realizing the
world is watching, he obliges, lifting Kitty into the air.

159   **EXT. METROPOLIS MUSEUM OF NATURAL HISTORY - SAME TIME**   159   *

A TOUR BUS pulls into frame.   *

159A **INT. METROPOLIS MUSEUM - ENTRANCE - MOMENTS LATER**   159A   *

A PLASTIC DONATION BOX, filled with cash, reads SUGGESTED   *
DONATION: TEN DOLLARS. A NICKEL is dropped in.   *

                              MUSEUM GUARD   *
                    I'm sorry sir, but we're closing   *
                    in ten minutes.   *

REVEAL LEX and his men strolling into the museum. They're   *
oddly dressed as TOURISTS. Stanford has a CAMERA CASE   *
around his neck.   *

                              LEX   *
                    We only need five.   *

Lex continues onward while checking his watch, as if   *
waiting for something.   *

160   **INT. METROPOLIS MUSEUM - DINOSAUR HALL - MOMENTS LATER**   160   *

Lex and the men pass one exhibit after another while BRUTUS   *
and GRANT break away down a flight of steps into...   *

160A   **INT. METROPOLIS MUSEUM - BASEMENT - CONTINUOUS**   160A   *

They turn another corner and find a BREAKER PANEL. They   *
open it, finding dozens of switches inside.   *

161   **INT. METROPOLIS MUSEUM - MINERAL EXHIBIT - CONTINUOUS**   161

Lex and Stanford continue into an exhibit of CRYSTALS and
GEMSTONES. Riley lingers for a brief moment, longingly   *
staring at A LARGE DIAMOND, but Lex pays no attention. He   *
enters...   *

162   **INT. METROPOLIS MUSEUM - METEORITE EXHIBIT - CONTINUOUS**   162

...a spectacular exhibit of METEORITES. They range in size,   *
shape, and color with the largest lit by a spotlight in the   *
center of the room. It seems very special, until Lex walks   *
right past it, turning his attention to a back wall full of   *
smaller rocks.   *

Lex checks his watch. Opening the camera case, Stanford   *
removes what looks like a pair of HI-TECH GOGGLES with   *
dials for RADIOACTIVE SENSITIVITY, HEAT, etc...   *

163   **INT. METROPOLIS MUSEUM - MAINTENANCE HALL - SAME TIME**   163   *

Brutus checks his watch while Grant finds a MAIN SWITCH in   *
the breaker panel.   *

164   **INT. METROPOLIS MUSEUM - METEORITE EXHIBIT - SAME TIME**   164   *

Stanford turns on the goggles, tunes a dial, and hands them   *
to Lex. He puts them on.   *

GOGGLE POV: Nothing shows up. Lex looks at his watch and   *
waits patiently, counting down to himself.   *

165   **EXT. METROPOLIS MUSEUM - MAINTENANCE HALL - SAME TIME**   165   *

Riley and Grant nod, then FLIP THE MAIN POWER SWITCH.   *

166   **INT. METROPOLIS MUSEUM, METEOR EXHIBIT - SAME TIME**   166

THE LIGHTS GO OUT. Other museum patrons gasp, but Lex and   *
his men don't move.   *

GOGGLE POV: Everything is in near darkness -- the   *
meteorites all appear in deep shades of blue.   *

Lex turns a dial on the side of the goggles, setting the   *
level of specific radiation.   *

GOGGLE POV: A single meteorite is suddenly ILLUMINATED by a   *
faint, shimmering green aura.   *

In shadows, Lex grins.   *

                         LEX   *
        Bingo.   *

In the darkness, we hear the sound of GLASS SHATTERING,   *
followed by a piercing ALARM.   *

166A   **INT. METROPOLIS MUSEUM, METEOR EXHIBIT - MOMENTS LATER**   166A   *

The lights come back on. Lex and his men are gone. The   *
museum visitors start making their way toward the exit, not   *
noticing that ONE OF THE METEORITES IS MISSING. The placard   *
where it once sat is marked ADIS ABABA, 1978.   *

167   **EXT. HOSPITAL - EMERGENCY ROOM ENTRANCE - LATER**   167   *

EMTs near an AMBULANCE gaze in wonder as Superman descends   *
with the "unconscious" Kitty in his arms. She slyly opens
one eye and checks her watch as they land.

                    SUPERMAN
          Alright Miss--

She abruptly wakes up and hops to her feet.

                    KITTY
          It's a miracle! My back, my heart
          palpitation -- healed! What did
          you do?

                    SUPERMAN
          Nothing, I just--

Kitty wraps her arms around him, squeezes tight. Beat. Her
mouth inches close to his ear.

                    KITTY
               (seductive)
          Call me Katherine.

                    SUPERMAN
          Katherine, I really should be
          going.

She eases off. Her hand slides down his back, copping a
feel.

                    KITTY
          Of course. Places to go, people
          to save...
               (looks around)
          I know this is so tacky, but do
          you want to maybe grab coffee
          sometime?

Kitty thinks better of it.

                    KITTY (CONT'D)
          I'm sorry. Forget I ever said
          that. Thanks for your help! Bye!

Kitty scampers off. Superman watches her leave, puzzled but
flattered, then launches into the air.

A173   **VIDEO FOOTAGE FILLS THE SCREEN:**   A173

Two WINDOW WASHERS hang precariously from the edge of a
broken platform on top of a large building, holding on for
dear life. In the foreground, a German reporter narrates
the unfolding disaster behind him.

                       GERMAN REPORTER (V.O.)   *
              Hallo. Hinter mir können Sie Se   *
              zwei Fensterunterlegscheiben   *
              hängen an für liebes Leben...   *

The window washing platform suddenly BREAKS and the window *
washers PLUMMET. WHOOSH! The reporter turns to see A RED   *
STREAK zip across the sky... and the window washers seem to *
DISAPPEAR.   *

The video cuts to the window washers, now being interviewed *
on the ground, their faces stained with tears.   *

                       GERMAN WINDOW WASHER
              Er speicherte mein Leben. Ich
              verdanke alles <u>Superman</u>!

173   **INT. DAILY PLANET - THE NEXT DAY**   173 *

Polly and Gil stare up at the television.

                          GIL   *
              It's like this on every channel.

He flips channels to prove his point. CLICK!   *

ON TELEVISION: We see BLURRY SECURITY CAMERA FOOTAGE: *

IN A SMALL HARDWARE STORE, a thief robs a cashier at   *
gunpoint. As the frames step forward, the man turns at   *
something off-screen and fires repeatedly.   *

One frame later, his gun is missing...   *
...the next frame has him entangled in power cords...   *
...then, SUPERMAN is shaking hands with the store owner.   *

CLICK! An anchor delivers the day's news underneath A MAP   *
that marks Superman's overnight feats with his trademark   *
'S'.   *

                       ANCHOR (V.O.)
              ...Reports flooding in from
              Metropolis, Houston, Gotham, and
              as far away as Cairo and
              Shanghai. This is just the latest   *
              in a series of overnight
              appearances by the Man of
              Steel...

CLICK! The channel changes and we see a home-video-camera-
shot WHIP PAN to a shot of the Eiffel Tower -- WHOOSH! A
RED STREAK tears across the sky -- tourists scream and take
excited pictures.   *

> BRITISH EXPERT (V.O.)
> Satellites have proven most
> ineffective at tracking him, with
> scientists telling us he is
> literally moving...

CLICK! In suburban Japan, a TANKER TRUCK is on fire.
Superman swoops in, easily blows it out, waves to the
camera, and flies off.

> JAPANESE REPORTER
> (SUBTITLED)
> ...faster than speeding bullets
> and more powerful than a
> locomotive.

WIDER: Reveal that all of the televisions in the office are
displaying footage of Superman's feats from the night
before.

CLARK enters to see that the office is transfixed by the
broadcasts. He glances up at one.

ON TELEVISION: OUTSIDE OF A DELI, TWO MEN are being lead
away by COPS while a reporter questions the DELI OWNER:

> MONTAGE REPORTER #3
> Sir, after he captured the men
> trying to rob your deli, did he
> do or say anything?

> DELI OWNER   *
> He tried the hummus. He said he   *
> liked it -- and Superman never   *
> lies!   *

Clark hides a smile and makes his way to Perry's office. He   *
passes by another broadcast: *

ON TELEVISION: PHOTOGRAPHS of Superman saving Kitty are   *
shown. We clearly see Superman holding up her car.   *

174   **INT. DAILY PLANET - PERRY'S OFFICE - DAY**   174   *

CLOSE ON: The SAME PHOTO, only Lois is holding this one.   *
She flips to another, moments later, of Superman carrying a   *
beautiful woman in his arms. We realize that it is KITTY   *
KOWALSKI. She seems jealous, but feigns boredom.   *

> LOIS
> Eh.

> PERRY
> Eh? EH!? That's iconic! And they
> were taken by a twelve year-old
> with a camera phone. Olsen,
> what've you got?

Jimmy hands him A PHOTO OF A SKYLINE. Jimmy points to a
small blur in the clouds.

>   JIMMY
>   He's right there, Chief. Look in
>   the sky.

>   LOIS
>   It's a bird.

>   PERRY
>   It's a plane.

>   JIMMY
>   No look, it's--

>   CLARK
>   You wanted to see me?

Clark stands in the doorway, holding a pad and pencil.

>   PERRY
>   Sit down, Kent. Let's talk about
>   some half-time strategy.

Lois knows where this is going. Clark watches her every
move.

>   PERRY (CONT'D)
>   Not long ago, Superman and the
>   Daily Planet went together like
>   bacon and eggs. Death and taxes.
>   Sigfreid and Roy!! Now I want
>   that bond back!
>   (beat)
>   Lois, I know you've been sneaking   *
>   around working on that blackout--   *

>   LOIS   *
>   It wasn't just a blackout, Chief!   *
>   It was cell phones, pagers,   *
>   automobiles, airplanes--   *

>   PERRY   *
>   --but every other paper in town   *
>   has their best looking female
>   reporters on rooftops waiting to
>   interview Superman, and none of
>   them have the history you two do.

>   LOIS
>   What? No! Chief, listen to me.
>   I've done Superman.
>   (correcting herself)
>   Covered him-- you know what I
>   mean.

                    PERRY
          Exactly! That makes you the
          expert, so you're going to do him
          again.

Clark tries to speak up, it's futile.

                    LOIS
          But there are a dozen other
          stories out there.

                    PERRY
          Name one!

                    LOIS
          Well... there was a museum
          robbery last night. Even Superman
          missed that one. He was too busy
          saving this... stripper!

She slaps the photos down. Clark seems surprised -- *I did?*

                    PERRY
          What'd they steal?

                    LOIS
          A meteorite.

                    PERRY
          Boring! Gil can handle it.

                    JIMMY
          Why don't you guys track down Lex
          Luthor?

Everyone turns to Jimmy.

                    JIMMY (CONT'D)
          No one's seen him since he won
          his fifth appeal, and he's got
          more bad history with Superman
          than anyone. Maybe he's got
          something to say.

                    PERRY
          Luthor's yesterday's news.   *

LOIS
No, I like that idea! Perry,
Lex Luthor is a career
criminal who nearly killed
him for God's sake! Just
because Lex doesn't fly --

CLARK
(whispers)
Jimmy... How'd Lex Luthor get
out prison?
                                                          *

LOIS
...what is this, a newspaper
or a tabloid? We have plenty
of gossip columnists equipped
to cover Superman...

JIMMY
(whispers)
The appeals court called
Superman as a witness. He
wasn't around. How much do
you think that pisses off
Superman now?

LOIS
...so give him to someone
else!
   (thinks)
Polly! Give him to Polly!

CLARK
(whispers)
A lot.

They look out at the bullpen. Polly just glares at them.

Perry draws the blinds. The discussion is over.   *

                    PERRY (CONT'D)   *
             (quietly)
          Lois? Super. Man.

                    LOIS
          What about the blackout?

                    PERRY
          Kent? Blackout.

                    LOIS
          Great. Thanks, Chief.

She storms out. Clark goes after her. Only Jimmy is left.

                    PERRY
          What are you standing around
          for?! You're a copy boy again if
          you don't bring me one decent
          picture of him this week.

                    JIMMY
          But Ch--

Perry holds up a finger.

                    JIMMY (CONT'D)
          I wasn't gonna say it.

175   **INT. DAILY PLANET - BULLPEN**   175

Clark follows Lois to her desk. She has her back to him.

                    CLARK
          Lois? I'm sorry, I didn't know--

                                LOIS
                Here.

She turns around, holding up a thick stack of FILES -- her
blackout research.

                                LOIS (CONT'D)
                Take it! You wanted a way out of
                the obits? Here you go.

                    CLARK
          No, not really. Not if it's going
          to bother--

                    LOIS
          Bother me? Of course not!

                    CLARK
               (takes the files)
          Oh good, because I'd hate it if
          this damaged our relationship

                    LOIS
          Relationship!?   *

Lois sees a TV displaying an image of SUPERMAN holding up a   *
chain of TWELVE MOUNTAIN CLIMBERS. She rolls her eyes.   *

                    JASON (O.S.)   *
          Mommy!

JASON runs into her arms. She sighs, smiles. Rubs his hair.

                    RICHARD
               (holds up a report card)
          He got an A in science, but a D
          in gym, so we're doing something
          right.

                    LOIS
          At least one of us is.

Richard notices Clark is holding Lois' research.

                    LOIS (CONT'D)
          It's Perry. He just shoved   *
          Superman back into my life.

                    RICHARD
          Well, honey, I'm sure you can   *
          find a way to interview Superman
          without bringing him back into
          your life.

ON TV, a reporter is surrounded by people with binoculars
and telescopes, waiting for Superman to pass overhead.

                    REPORTER (ON TV)
          There's really no way around it,
          folks. Superman is back in all of
          our lives!

Richard sighs and tries a different approach:

                         RICHARD
               How about this -- We'll stay late,
               get dinner -- I'll help with
               Superman, and you and Clark can
               work on the blackout... together.

Jason's inhaler wheezes, nearly empty. Lois instinctively
pulls a new one out of her purse and hands it to him. She
exhales and calms down.

                         RICHARD (CONT'D)
               Is that good for you, Clark?

                         CLARK
               Sounds swell!

Beat. Lois and Richard look at him. *Did he just say swell?*

                         JASON
               Look, mom, I got my flu shot!

                         LOIS
               Did it hurt?

                         JASON
               Not a bit!

                         LOIS
               That's my boy.

177   **INT. YACHT - MAIN CABIN - MOMENTS LATER**   177

Classical music blares. Lex stares up at the NAUTICAL MAP on   *
the wall for a moment, then looks down at another map rolled   *
up in his hands. He starts to unroll it when he hears the   *
click-clack of Kitty's shoes behind him. He smiles and turns   *
just as she SLAPS HIM. Hard.   *

                         KITTY
               I was gonna pretend my brakes were
               out! Like we talked about! *Pretend*!
               You didn't have to actually cut
               them!

                         LEX
               Of course I did. A man can always
               tell when a woman is pretending.
               Especially Superman.

She tries to slap him again, but Lex catches her arm. She
tries to pull away but he won't let go. Lex casts her a stern
glare. She backs down.

                         KITTY
               Did you get your dumb rock?

Lex nods and smiles. Seductive. They move closer, like this is some twisted flirtation.

                    LEX   *
          I did. Now ask me about the map.   *

She looks at the map on the wall.   *

                    KITTY   *
          That map?   *

                    LEX   *
          No. This one.   *

He holds up the rolled map in his hands.   *

                    LEX (CONT'D)   *
          This map... is the future.   *

They move CLOSER -- as if about to kiss, when: *

                    GRANT (ON INTERCOM)   *
          Mr. Luthor, they're about to start!

Lex is clearly annoyed by the intrusion.

                    LEX
          Thank you, Grant.
               (then)
          Duty calls, Ms. Kowalski. We'll
          talk more about this later.

He puts the tube away and glances down at his desk -- at a   *
NEWSPAPER.   *

                    LEX (CONT'D)
          Nice picture.

He leaves. Winded, Kitty leans against the wall and looks down to see the photo of her with Superman on the FRONT PAGE. She GRINS, not noticing something else:

ON LEX'S COMPUTER are theoretical renderings of Kryptonian crystal technology -- including vehicles and land masses.

178   **INT. YACHT - BRIDGE - MOMENTS LATER**   178

A MISSILE lays on a counter, partially dismantled. Stanford is in the midst of carefully removing the EXPLOSIVE. He places it into a drawer, when Lex enters.

Stanford measures the missile compartment, then turns his attention to THE ROCKY METEORITE stolen from the museum. WHACK! He chips off pieces of the outer shell. Lex peers down at the meteorite's inner layer.

A FAINT GREEN GLOW appears inside: KRYPTONITE. Stanford is
amazed for a moment, then chips away more.

A LONG SHARP SLIVER OF KRYPTONITE breaks off onto the
counter. Lex eyes it, curiously, then picks it up and slips
it into his pocket.

Stanford carefully places the remaining chunk of kryptonite
into the metal vice, just under the drill. He looks to Lex,
who nods. The drill revs to life. Stanford lowers it, and
just as the tip starts drilling into the kryptonite --

                                                    CUT TO:

179   **INT. DAILY PLANET - BULLPEN - THAT NIGHT**   179

The office is quieter and mostly empty. Just a few
stragglers. JIMMY is at a computer, going through various
photos. All of them show blurry shapes and streaks.

> JIMMY
> Crap.

> CLARK
> What's wrong?

Clark is at the nearby water cooler.

> JIMMY
> The guy just moves too fast. I
> haven't gotten one decent shot.

> CLARK
> Keep at it. He's got to slow down
> eventually.

CLANG! Clark turns, sees JASON wearing a trash can on his   *
head, rampaging around the office like a giant monster. He
slams into a pole but keeps on going.

> JASON
> RAAAAAAAAARRRRR!

> CLARK
> Jimmy, is he... okay?

> JIMMY
> Yeah, he's fine. A few weird
> allergies, asthma-- but the kid's
> come a long way since he was
> born.

> CLARK
> What do you mean?

> JIMMY
> Well...
>> (quieter)
> Miss Lane doesn't like to talk
> about it, but Jason was born a
> little premature. They weren't
> sure if he was even going to make
> it.   *

Jimmy spots something on the computer.   *

> JIMMY (CONT'D)   *
> GOT HIM!   *

He excitedly zooms into a photo of a skyscraper. Sighs.   *

                         JIMMY (CONT'D)
                Nevermind. Just a bat.

ON THE OTHER SIDE OF THE BULLPEN

A MAP OF THE EAST COAST is sprawled on Lois' desk. She's
noting the TIMES and places that the blackout was recorded.
Using these times, she's drawn a series of concentric
circles, getting closer to the origin point of the
blackout.

                         LOIS
                Weird. If these times are right,
                it looks like the blackout spread
                from a specific origin point.

                         RICHARD
                Where?

                         LOIS
                I'm not sure yet.

Richard sits across from her, flipping through piles of old
articles and research about Superman.

                         RICHARD
                So with the superhearing, does he
                hear each sound by itself, or
                everything all at once?

                         LOIS   *
                Both.

Across the room, Clark PERKS UP, listening to them...

                         RICHARD
                He's certainly a lot taller than
                I thought.

                         LOIS
                Six-four.   *

                         RICHARD
                I love that he can see through
                anything. I'd have fun with that.

                         LOIS
                   (smirks)   *
                Anything but lead.

                         RICHARD   *
                And what's that other thing he   *
                does with his eyes? Laser blasts,   *
                or--   *

                         LOIS   *
                Heat vision. And he doesn't use   *
                it much.   *

                         RICHARD   *
          I bet he's--   *

                         LOIS
               (miss know-it-all)
          Two hundred and twenty five
          pounds, faster than a speeding
          bullet, invulnerable to anything
          but Kryptonite, and he never
          lies.

                         RICHARD
          Kryptonite?

                         LOIS
          Radioactive pieces of his
          homeworld. It's deadly... to him.

                         RICHARD
          Wow. Sounds like the perfect guy.

Richard looks at Clark, then at a photo of Superman.

                         RICHARD (CONT'D)
               (whispers)
          Hey, how tall would you say Clark
          is?

                         LOIS
          I don't know, maybe six-three,   *
          six-four.   *

                         RICHARD
          Around two hundred pounds?

                         LOIS
          Sure, why?

She looks at Richard. Richard looks at Clark. Lois and
Richard BOTH look at Clark. Wondering...

IN THE BACKGROUND: Clark looks up, smiles nervously. They
both laugh to themselves. Richard stands up and kisses her
on the head. Smiles.

                         RICHARD
          Jimmy, Jason -- let's go get
          these intrepid reporters
          something to keep them going,
          okay?

                         JASON
          Burrrrritos! RAAARRR!

Jimmy and Jason join him and they leave the room. Their
absence creates an uncomfortable silence. Just Lois and
Clark. Alone. He keeps stealing glances, trying to come up
with something to say. Surprisingly, she beats him to it:

                              LOIS
                    So. Have you found a place to
                    live yet?

                              CLARK
                    No. I'm still looking.

                              LOIS
                    Where've you been spending your
                    nights?

                              CLARK
                    Oh... here and there. You know,   *
                    Lois -- I wanted to ask you about   *
                    that article--   *

                              LOIS   *
                         (cutting him off)   *
                    Hey, I'm gonna run downstairs for   *
                    some fresh air. Let's talk when I   *
                    get back.   *

          She grabs her purse, spilling things all over the floor:
          MAKE-UP, a small tape recorder, and a PACK OF CIGARETTES.   *
          She looks up at Clark, momentarily embarrassed, then   *
          gathers everything up, absentmindedly stuffing the tape   *
          recorder into her coat pocket. She darts for the door.   *
          Clark watches her get into an elevator, and lowers his
          glasses.

          X-RAY POV: Lois in the elevator, but it's going UP, not
          DOWN. He smiles, then looks at an open window.

180   **EXT. DAILY PLANET ROOF - NIGHT**   180

          A BIRD'S EYE VIEW of the Daily Planet roof. The large
          illuminated GLOBE seems to light up the sky.

          CAMERA DESCENDS onto LOIS, standing against a ledge. She
          looks over her shoulder, making sure she's alone, then
          removes a cigarette from her purse and smiles. It's been a
          long time. She flicks a lighter, but just as she touches it
          to the cigarette, VWOOSH! the flame is blown out.

          Lois tries again. It goes out again. Annoyed, she flicks
          the lighter harder and it drops out of her hand. She kneels
          down, looking for it.

                              SUPERMAN (O.S.)
                    You know, you really shouldn't
                    smoke, Miss Lane.

          SHE YELPS and looks up. SUPERMAN is landing on the ledge.

                              SUPERMAN (CONT'D)
                    I didn't mean to--

                    LOIS
          I'm fine. Really. I just wasn't
          expecting... *you*.

She straightens up, composes herself. He steps closer. She   *
steps back. It's awkward.   *

          LOIS   SUPERMAN
     So, where--   I'm--

Beat.

                    LOIS (CONT'D)
          You first.

                    SUPERMAN
          I'm sorry. For leaving like that.
               (beat)
          With all the press on the plane I
          wasn't sure if it was the best
          time for us to talk.

Beat. Lois is confused, then realizes: *

                    LOIS   *
          Oh right. The plane. Well,   *
          there's no press around now --   *
          except me.   *

                    SUPERMAN   *
          I know people are asking a lot of   *
          questions, now that I'm back, and   *
          I think it's only fair that I   *
          answer... those people.   *

                    LOIS
               (disbelief)
          So you're here for... an
          interview?

He nods.

                    LOIS (CONT'D)
          Okay then. An interview it is.

She reaches into her purse, looking for the TAPE RECORDER.
He looks her over.

                    LOIS (CONT'D)
          Where did I put that thing...

                    SUPERMAN
          Right pocket.   *

                         LOIS
          Huh?

                         SUPERMAN
          The tape recorder. It's in your   *
          right pocket.   *

Lois just smiles. She turns the tape recorder on.

                         LOIS
          Let's start with the big
          question. Where did you go?

                         SUPERMAN
          To Krypton.

                         LOIS
          But you told me it was destroyed.
          Ages ago.

                         SUPERMAN
          I did. It was. But when   *
          astronomers thought they found   *
          it... I had to see for myself.   *

Beat. Lois seems genuinely affected by that.

                    LOIS
Well you're back, and everyone
seems to be happy about it.

                    SUPERMAN
Not everyone.
        (beat)
I read the article, Lois. 'Why
the World Doesn't Need Superman'.

                    LOIS
So did a lot of people. Tomorrow
night they're giving me the
Pulitzer for it--

                    SUPERMAN
Why did you write it?

Lois clicks the tape recorder OFF and turns away. She's   *
hiding tears.   *

                    LOIS   *
How could you leave me like that?   *

Beat. He's caught off guard.   *

                    SUPERMAN   *
I'm sorry if I hurt you--   *

                    LOIS   *
No. The time to say sorry was   *
five years ago.   *

She wipes the tears from her eyes. She is NOT going to cry.   *

                    LOIS (CONT'D)   *
I moved on. I had to. And so did   *
the rest of us. That's why I   *
wrote it. The world doesn't need   *
a saviour.   *

Superman is heartbroken.   *

                    SUPERMAN   *
Lois, will you come with me?   *

                    LOIS   *
Why?   *

                    SUPERMAN   *
There's something I want to show   *
you. Please.   *

                    LOIS   *
I--   *

                    SUPERMAN   *
Please.   *

Beat. She's obviously hesitant.   *

                    LOIS   *
          I can't be gone long.   *

                    SUPERMAN   *
          You won't be.   *

She finally steps closer and kicks off her heels, then   *
places her feet on top of his. Looks up into his eyes.   *

                    LOIS   *
          Clark says the reason you left   *
          without saying goodbye is because   *
          it was too unbearable for you.   *
              (beat)   *
          Personally, I think that's a load   *
          of crap.   *

                    SUPERMAN   *
          Clark?   *

                    LOIS   *
          A guy I work with.   *

                    SUPERMAN   *
          Maybe Clark's right.   *

She's staring into his eyes - remembering, but trying to   *
stay strong.   *

                    LOIS   *
          You know, my... um... Richard, is   *
          a pilot. He takes me up all the   *
          time.   *

                    SUPERMAN   *
          Not like this.   *

She looks down and GASPS, suddenly realizing they're already fifty feet over the rooftop and moving over the edge.

One of her feet slips off of his -- she grabs on tighter. So does he. They rise higher, past the clouds, until the city becomes a cluster of lights. Lois closes her eyes, memories flooding back.

He smiles, and they finally stop high above the city.

181   **EXT. SKY - CONTINUOUS**   181

It's totally silent and still. Lois looks around in awe.

                    SUPERMAN
          What do you hear?

                    LOIS
          Nothing. It's quiet.

                    SUPERMAN
          Do you know what I hear? I hear
          everything.
                    (beat)
          You wrote that the world doesn't
          need a savior -- but every day I
          hear people crying for one.

For once, Lois is speechless. Superman smiles gently.

                    SUPERMAN (CONT'D)
          I'll take you back now.

182   **EXT. RIVER - NIGHT**   182   *

SUPERMAN AND LOIS appear over a blanket of stars. But then   *
something strange happens -- Superman reaches out and seems   *
to TOUCH the starfield. It magically RIPPLES under his   *
touch, and we realize it was just a reflection. They're   *
flying only a few inches over the RIVER.   *

They fly past rows of shore homes. Lois catches a glimpse   *
of her own house as they zip by, heading towards--   *

183   **EXT. METROPOLIS BRIDGE - MOMENTS LATER**   183   *

A sprawling steel arch structure, beautifully lit. We   *
follow a car heading towards the city, but then dip BELOW   *
THE BRIDGE to find Superman and Lois flying under the   *
structure.   *

They glide past a section of SCAFFOLDING where SPARKS from   *
blowtorches rain down like fireworks. Several CONSTRUCTION   *
WORKERS turn and gawk as they continue flying towards the   *
city.   *

184   **EXT. SKIES OVER METROPOLIS - MOMENTS LATER**   184   *

Even at night, Metropolis' majestic towers are bathed in
golden light. Superman and Lois soar over and between them,
lights shimmering on their faces.

He pulls to the right and takes her straight towards a tall   *
building. Lois braces in fear, but they quickly jet
upwards. He pulls her close, and they slowly turn and spin,
wrapped in each other's arms as they rise upward. It's like
a slowdance in the middle of the air.

They rise past the BULLPEN window. Superman and Lois reach
the top of the building. THE DAILY PLANET globe appears
behind them.

185   **EXT. DAILY PLANET - ROOFTOP**   185

THEY LAND gently on the roof. Lois looks deeply into his
eyes, faces just inches apart. They both can see it coming.
This is the moment. Lois begins to MOVE CLOSER -- and just
as her lips are about to touch his... Lois abruptly pulls
away.

                    LOIS
          Richard's a good man. And you've
          been gone a long time.

                    SUPERMAN
          I know.

She walks back to the rooftop door and turns around.

                    LOIS
          So will I still see you? Around?

                    SUPERMAN
          I'm always around. Goodnight,
          Lois.

He turns, about to take off again...

                    LOIS
          Wait...

Beat. She looks as if she wants to say something else.
Something important.

                    LOIS (CONT'D)
          Nevermind. Goodnight.

And with that, Superman rises into the air and flies off.
Lois watches until he's gone, then takes a deep breath.

187   **INT. DAILY PLANET - CONFERENCE ROOM - CONTINUOUS**   187   *

Richard, Jason, Clark, and Jimmy are in the conference room   *
eating take-away. Richard looks up to see Lois enter, dazed   *
and frazzled.   *

                    RICHARD   *
          We've got beef, honey -- do you   *
          want the veggie or tofu wrap?   *

                    LOIS   *
          Honey beef.   *

                    RICHARD
          What?

She snaps out of it.

                    LOIS
          Sorry. Veggie. I'll have the
          veggie wrap.

Richard stares, sees her wind-blown hair. Clark watches
their exchange.

                    RICHARD
          Lois, where have you been?

                    LOIS
          I was just on the roof, getting
          some air.

She smiles, trying to finesse the interaction. He looks at her, even more suspicious than before.

> RICHARD
> Tell me the truth, Lois.

She trembles, nervous.

> RICHARD (CONT'D)
> Have you been smoking?

187A **INT. DAILY PLANET - BULLPEN - THE NEXT DAY**   187A

WHOOSH! PAGES come out of a printer and are immediately grabbed by a female hand. We get a glimpse of the ARTICLE as the pages move through the Daily Planet -- it's an INTERVIEW with SUPERMAN.

We FOLLOW the pages...

188   **INT. DAILY PLANET - PERRY'S OFFICE - CONTINUOUS**   188

...as they LAND on a DESK. Perry's desk. He picks it up and takes a single glance at it -- and up at Lois.

> PERRY
> Is this real?

Lois just stares at him. It's real.

> PERRY (CONT'D)
> How'd you find him?

> LOIS
> He found me.

> PERRY
> Great. I can't wait to read--

> LOIS
> (sweetly)
> So, *Mr. White*. About that
> blackout...

> PERRY
> Lois, this is the biggest night
> of your life. Have you picked out   *
> a dress? Something *snazzy* I...   *

> LOIS
> It just feels a little weird,
> winning for that article. It
> doesn't seem right anymore.

                    PERRY
          What doesn't seem right?

                    LOIS
          Getting an award for an article
          called 'Why the world doesn't
          need Superman.'
                    (holds up the newspaper)
          When according to *this* paper,
          they do!

                    PERRY
          Lois, Pulitzer Prizes are like
          Academy Awards. Nobody remembers
          what you got one for. Just that
          you got one.

                    LOIS
          But--

                    PERRY
          This night's for you, Lois. Just
          enjoy it. I'm sure Kent's on the
          blackout.

189   **EXT. ARCTIC SKIES - SAME TIME**   189

VWOOSH! Superman soars through a dark and overcast sky.   *
TIGHT on his face -- we begin to hear...   *

                    SUPERMAN (V.O.)   *
          Father...   *

NORTHERN LIGHTS shimmer in the grey sky. Superman soars
through them...

                    SUPERMAN (V.O.) (CONT'D)   *
          It's been a long time since I've   *
          come to you...   *

...and moves towards something on the distance...   *

                    SUPERMAN (V.O.) (CONT'D)   *
          But I've never felt so alone.   *

190   **EXT. FORTRESS OF SOLITUDE - SAME TIME**   190

The massive fortress of solitude sits on the ice below.   *

191   **INT. FORTRESS OF SOLITUDE - SAME TIME**   191   *

Superman lands inside his fortress. It is dark.   *

He approaches the console. The crystal has been taken. WITH
A VOICE ECHOING THROUGH THE ARCTIC LIKE THUNDER:

                                          SUPERMAN
            FATHER!?!

VWOOSH! He rockets straight up and out of the fortress.

192   **INT. DAILY PLANET - BULLPEN - LATER**   192

Jimmy darts across the office, carrying TWO GOWNS on
hangers. He rushes to Lois, who is on the phone.

                             LOIS (ON PHONE)
                  Department of Water & Power
                  please.

Jimmy holds up the two gowns. She points to the blue one.
He hangs it on a coat rack behind her desk.

                             LOIS (CONT'D)
                  Hi, this is Lois Lane from the
                  Daily Planet, I was wondering if--
                      (beat; rolls her eyes)
                  Yes, he is a very nice man-- But
                  I was wondering if I could ask
                  you a few more questions about
                  the blackout...

Jimmy re-appears holding a DRY ERASE BOARD that reads: *

                  RICHARD'S LATE -- TUX NOT READY AT CLEANERS.   *
                      CAN YOU PICK UP JASON FROM SCHOOL?   *

She nods and waves Jimmy away.   *

                             LOIS (CONT'D)   *
                  I already spoke to the Technology   *
                  and Energy Committee and they   *
                  sent me back to you and now   *
                  you're sending me back to them?   *
                      (beat)   *
                  The who? Okay. Can I get *their*   *
                  number?   *

MOMENTS LATER: *

                             LOIS (CONT'D)   *
                  Metropolis Public Works? My name   *
                  is Lois Lane, I'm calling from   *
                  the -- yes, I'll hold.   *

MOMENTS LATER: *

                             LOIS (CONT'D)   *
                  ...Uh huh. Stephen Jones. And he   *
                  does what?   *
                      (beat)   *
                  Deputy Director of the Power   *
                  Outage Task Force... Great.   *
                  Thanks.   *

MOMENTS LATER: *

> LOIS (CONT'D)
> Hi Stephen, this is Lois Lane
> from the Daily Planet. I'm
> writing an investigative article
> on the blackout and just need a
> little info on a few outstanding
> power grids...

192 B   **INT. DAILY PLANET - CLOSET - LATER**   192 B

While on her mobile phone, Lois now has her gown on and is
putting on a pair of earrings and shoes.

> LOIS (ON PHONE)
> So the uptown grid went dark at
> 12:36, and mid-town ten seconds
> before. So which grid was hit
> first?

> VOICE (ON PHONE)
> Grid J-12 across the river. The
> Vanderworth property.

> LOIS (ON PHONE)
> You're sure. Nothing before that?

> VOICE (ON PHONE)
> That's it.

> VOICE ON PHONE
> Thank you very much.

She hangs up and dials again, staring at the map of
METROPOLIS.

> LOIS
> Information please. I need a
> listing for Vanderworth.
>   (beat)
> 6 Springwood Drive. Is that a
> business or a residence?
>   (beat)
> A residence. Thank you.

She pulls the map off of the bulletin board. Lois looks at
the clock on the wall -- and panics.

> LOIS (CONT'D)
> Jason!

193   **EXT. SCHOOL - AFTERNOON**   193

Jason stands outside with a TEACHER. A CAR pulls up. It's
Lois. She honks and waves.

                    LOIS
              Get in!

Jason toddles over and jumps into the car. The teacher
bends down, waving at Lois through the window.

                    TEACHER
              Congratulations, Miss Lane. Say
              hi to Superman for me!

                    LOIS
                 (smiling politely)
              Thanks.

194   **OMITTED**   194   *

195/196 **EXT. VANDERWORTH ESTATE - DRIVEWAY - LATER**   195/196   *

The car comes to a stop. Jason looks out the car window at   *
the Vanderworth mansion.

                    JASON
              Mommy, where are we? Is this the   *
              Pulitzer?   *

                    LOIS
              No. I just needs to ask these   *
              people a few questions and then
              we can go.

She turns off the car and the sound of the radio dies, but   *
they can still hear something -- MUSIC -- but it's not   *
coming from the house. She looks out the window to see THE   *
YACHT docked on the shore.   *

Her CELL PHONE RINGS, displaying the name <u>DAILY PLANET</u>. She   *
looks at it, then tosses the phone in the glove box. Lois   *
gets out of the car.   *

                    JASON   *
              Can I stay in the car?   *

                    LOIS   *
              Not on your life.   *

198   **INT. YACHT - ENTRANCE**   198   *

Lois and Jason quietly walk on board, stepping over empty
beer bottles and pizza boxes. They hear OPERA MUSIC but no
one seems to be around.

                    JASON
          Are we trespassing?

                    LOIS
          Yes. No. I mean 'shh'.

199   **INT. YACHT - CORRIDOR - CONTINUOUS**   199

Following the music, Lois and Jason descend a staircase and
enter a long corridor. The music abruptly stops. She spots
a doorway ahead, slightly ajar.

199A   **INT. YACHT - WARDROBE ROOM**   199A

They enter a room filled with fine suits, shoes, jewelry
and other expensive items. Lois looks at everything,
perplexed.

                    JASON (O.S.)
          I like the curly one.

Jason is pointing at something on a shelf. Lois looks at
it, and her eyes suddenly WIDEN in fear:

IT'S A MANNEQUIN'S HEAD. Wearing a TOUPEE. It's just one of
many, all neatly lined up in rows.

>   LOIS
>   (quietly)
>   Oh no.

She backs away, staring at the wigs. Terrified.

>   JASON
>   Mommy, what's wrong?

>   LOIS
>   Oh no. No no no...

THE ENTIRE ROOM suddenly jolts. We hear the ship's engine rumble. Lois runs to a small window and looks outside.

THROUGH THE WINDOW, we see the ship pulling away from shore.

>   LOIS (CONT'D)
>   This was a bad idea. Come on,   *
>   we've got to get out of here.

Lois grabs Jason and rushes to the door, but just as she opens it, she SHRIEKS. She's face to face with LEX LUTHOR: BALD, wearing a bathrobe, with a TOOTHBRUSH in his mouth.   *

>   LOIS (CONT'D)
>   Lex Luthor?

>   LEX
>   (toothbrush in mouth)
>   Lois Lane...

200   **INT. YACHT - MAIN ROOM - MOMENTS LATER**   200

Lois and Jason sit in the middle of the lavish room, surrounded by the thugs and Kitty. Now dressed and in one   *
of his wigs, Lex paces around them, staring at Jason...   *

>   LEX
>   And what's your name?

>   JASON
>   I'm not supposed to talk to
>   strangers.

>   LEX
>   Cute kid. Smart too.

>   LOIS
>   Thanks.

>   LEX
>   But I'm not really a stranger, am
>   I? I mean, this is like a little
>   reunion.
>   (MORE)

                         LEX (CONT'D)
          Heck, I'm a fan, Miss Lane! I
          love your writing!
                    (looking her over)
          And your dress.

                         LOIS
          I love your ship. How'd you get
          it? Swindle some old widow out of
          her money?

Kitty laughs. Lex's eyes narrow.

                         LEX
          Hey, didn't you win the Pulitzer
          prize for my favorite article
          "Why the World Doesn't Need
          Superman?"

                         LOIS
                    (glances at her watch)
          Not yet. Didn't you have a few
          more years to go on your double
          life sentence?   *

                         LEX   *
          Well, we can thank the Man of   *
          Steel for that. He's really good   *
          at *SWOOPING* in and catching the   *
          bad guys. But he's not so hot on   *
          the little things, like Miranda   *
          rights, due process -- *making   *
          your court date...*   *

Lois processes the information.

                         LOIS
          Did you have anything to do with
          the blackout?

Lex's eyes light up.

                         LEX
          Are you fishing for an interview,
          Miss Lane?

                        LOIS
          It's been a while since you were
          a headline. Maybe it's time
          people knew your name again.
                   (pulling Jason closer)
          How about we turn the boat
          around, call a cab for my son...
          and then you can do whatever you
          want with me.

Beat. Lex considers his options. Kitty theatrically opens
the Daily Planet paper with the photo of her and Superman
on the cover -- and *pretends* to read. Lois sees the photo
and realizes "the stripper" is Kitty. Annoyed, she rolls
her eyes. Lex spots a pad and pencil near A FAX MACHINE. He
looks at Jason.

                        LEX
          Do you know what posthumous
          means?

                        JASON
          No.

                        LEX
          Good.
                   (to Lois)
          Sorry, Miss. Lane -- we won't be
          turning around, but we do have
          some time to kill, so how about
          that interview?

He hands her the pad and pencil.

                        LEX (CONT'D)
          Your tools?

                                              CUT TO:

A PHOTOGRAPH OF LOIS AND JASON.

201   **INT. DAILY PLANET - BULLPEN - LATE AFTERNOON**   201   *

Jimmy is in a forlorn daze, staring at the photo. Behind
him, Clark walks in, UNNERVED.

                        CLARK
          Jimmy, can I take a look at any
          other information Lois collected
          on the blackout?

He sees Jimmy's expression.

                        CLARK (CONT'D)
          What's wrong?

                         JIMMY
            Lois and Jason are missing.

Jimmy turns to Perry's office, where he and Richard, both
wearing tuxedos, are pacing, upset and nervous.

202   **INT. DAILY PLANET - PERRY'S OFFICE - CONTINUOUS**   202

                         PERRY
            So what'd the school say?

                         RICHARD
            She picked Jason up at 4:40.

Clark enters.

                         CLARK
            I heard the news. What can I do?

                         PERRY
            We've tried her cell, but there's
            no answer and we're supposed to
            be at the ceremony in a half
            hour. You're a reporter, Clark --
            help Richard track her down.

ANGLE ON: Richard and Clark looking at each other,
perplexed.

202A   **INT. YACHT - MAIN CABIN - SAME TIME**   202A

                         LEX
            What do you know about crystals?

                         LOIS
            They make great chandeliers.

Lex drops a book in her lap. Lois flips through the book.   *
The images correspond to what he's saying. She looks up to
see Lex holding the WHITE CRYSTAL stolen from the Fortress
of Solitude.

                         LEX   *
            This crystal may seem
            unremarkable, but so is the seed
            of a redwood tree.
                    (MORE)

                         LEX (CONT'D)
                    It's how our mutual friend in
                    tights made his Arctic getaway
                    spot. Cute, but a little small
                    for my taste.

Lex points to a spot on A LARGE ANTIQUE NAUTICAL MAP that   *
has been modified to show A NEW LAND MASS off the coast of   *
Metropolis.

                         LOIS
                       (stunned)
                    You're building an...island?

                         LEX
                    You're not seeing the big
                    picture, Miss Lane. Here, let me
                    enlarge it for you.

He yanks down ANOTHER NAUTICAL MAP that shows THE LAND MASS   *
even larger than before -- nearly the size of a continent.   *

                         LEX (CONT'D)
                    It's not just an island. It's an
                    entirely new continent. Virtually
                    indestructible and self-
                    sustaining. For lack of a better
                    name, it's Krypton. An extinct
                    world, reborn on our own.

                         LOIS
                    Why?   *

                         LEX
                    Land, Miss Lane.
                       (beat)
                    Kitty, what did my father once   *
                    say to me?   *

                         KITTY   *
                    Get out?   *

                         LEX   *
                    Before that. He said, 'You can   *
                    print money, manufacture
                    diamonds, and people are a dime a
                    dozen, but they'll always need
                    land.'   *
                       (beat)
                    It's the one thing they don't   *
                    make any more of.   *

                         LOIS
                    But the United States government--   *

Lex yanks down yet another antique map that shows the new   *
continent has spread over half of North America, with all   *
the areas around it covered by water.   *

                    LEX
          --will be underwater. Simple
          logic, Miss Lane. Two objects
          simply can't occupy the same
          space.

                    LOIS
          And you think the rest of the
          world will just let you keep it?
          They'll--

                    LEX
          They'll what? I'll have alien
          technology...

Lex uses his fingers to make mocking 'alien antennae', then
turns suddenly COLD.

                    LEX (CONT'D)
          ADVANCED alien technology,
          thousands of years beyond what
          anyone else can throw at me.
          Weapons, vehicles, you name it.
               (beat)
          And eventually, the rest of the
          world will be begging me for a
          piece of this "high-tech beach-
          front property". In fact, they'll
          pay through the nose for it.

                    LOIS
          But millions of people will die.

                    LEX
          BILLIONS! Once again, the press
          underestimates me. This is front
          page news, Miss Lane!

Lois is speechless. So is Kitty -- this is the first time
she's heard his entire plan, and she doesn't seem to like
it.

                    LEX (CONT'D)
          Come on, say it.

                    LOIS
          You're insane.

                    LEX
          No, not that! Come on? It's just
          dangling off the tip of your
          tongue. SAY IT!

                        LEX   *
             Superman will never let you--

                        LEX (CONT'D)
             WRONG!!

Lex picks up the METAL BOX on the mantel. Opens it. A green
glow washes over his face.

                        LOIS
             What is that?

                        LEX
             I think you know exactly what
             this is.

He walks closer, shows it to her: THE KRYPTONITE. It has
been sheared to a sleek arrow-dynamic form, with a hole in
the center. Beat. She reaches for it but Lex snaps the box
shut.

                        LEX (CONT'D)
             Mind over muscle, Miss Lane. Mind
             over...   *

Beat. As Lex stares them down, something suddenly triggers   *
in his mind -- and he instantly becomes sinister.   *

                        LEX (CONT'D)   *
             Who's his father?!   *

Lex gets up and walks towards Lois, glaring...   *

                        LOIS   *
                 (quiet, under her   *
                  breath)   *
             Richard.   *

The INTERCOM CRACKLES: *

                        GRANT (ON INTERCOM)   *
             Mr. Luthor, we're approaching the   *
             coordinates.   *

                        LEX   *
                 (to Lois)   *
             You're sure?   *

                        GRANT (ON INTERCOM)
             Yes, sir. Latitude thirty-nine
             degrees north, and longitude
             seventy-one degrees west.

Without taking his eyes off of Lois, Lex walks to the   *
mantle, and picks up the KRYPTONITE BOX. Jason nervously   *
touches the keys. Lex comes back, stands next to him. He   *
looks from Jason to the Kryptonite... wondering. But Jason   *
doesn't react at all. Bothered, Lex walks to the stairs,   *
looks back at Lois.   *

                         LEX   *
                     (to Brutus)   *
            Don't let them out of this room.   *

      Brutus nods. Just after Lex exits, Lois scribbles something   *
      down on her notepad: *39°N, 71°W.*   *

203-204 **OMITTED**   203-204

205   **EXT. ATLANTIC OCEAN - DAY**   205

      Under an overcast sky, the yacht slows to a stop. FAR IN
      THE DISTANCE, Metropolis is just a speck on the horizon.

                                                              *

206   **EXT. YACHT - DECK - SAME TIME**   206

Lex and Kitty walk onto the deck and approach Grant, who is
setting up the modified ROCKET LAUNCHER. Riley is taping.

Lex removes the KRYPTONITE from one box, then the CRYSTAL
from another. Carefully, he inserts the crystal into the
kryptonite enclosure. There's a brief PULSE OF LIGHT as the
two objects from Krypton are brought together. Lex smiles.

                    LEX
          This is gonna be good.

Kitty watches everything, increasingly worried.

207   **INT. YACHT - MAIN ROOM - SAME TIME**   207

Lois stands in the middle of the room, nervous and upset.
Jason sits quietly at the piano, and after an awkward
moment of silence, starts to play HEART AND SOUL again.

Curious, Brutus approaches and sits down next to Jason. He
watches the boy play, and just as Lex did earlier, starts
to play along. Only he's terrible at piano.

Realizing Brutus is distracted, Lois slowly makes her way
toward the fax machine near Lex's desk.

BRUTUS continues playing. He doesn't notice as Lois scrawls
a message on the notepad, underneath the coordinates: *HELP
US! LOIS LANE.*

With her hands behind her back, she slides the paper into
the fax machine, then presses a button on the dial pad. IT
BEEPS. Worried, she glances over to Brutus. He didn't hear
it.

Carefully using the music to drown out the BEEPS, she dials
the number and presses SEND. It starts to CONNECT.

208   **INT. YACHT - DECK - SAME TIME**   208

Lex finishes securing the crystal/kryptonite into the
modified rocket, then inserts it into the launcher and
steps back.

                    STANFORD
          Ready, boss?

Lex nods. BOOM! STANFORD FIRES, blasting the rocket through
the air.

209   **EXT. ATLANTIC OCEAN - SAME TIME**   209

VWOOSH! The rocket sails through the sky before arcing
downward and smashing into the water. It disappears under
the surface with a slight GLOW.

210   **INT. YACHT - MAIN ROOM - SAME TIME**   210

THE LIGHTS FLICKER. ZAP! THE FAX MACHINE DIES before the
message goes through. Lois almost screams with frustration.
Jason and Brutus stop playing. They look around, confused.

211   **EXT. YACHT - DECK - SAME TIME**   211

The power on the ship dies. Lex and his men put on
binoculars. Kitty puts on designer sun glasses. Using
binoculars, Lex watches the ocean and smiles, thrilled.

213   **INT. DAILY PLANET - BULLPEN - LOIS' DESK - SAME TIME** 213

Richard and Clark are at Lois' desk, turning on her   *
computer.   *

                    CLARK
          Maybe she's at the burger shop on
          Mercer Street.

                    RICHARD
          She's a vegetarian.

                    CLARK
          Well, where's Jason's school? And   *
          wait, she is? Since when?   *

                    RICHARD   *
          Three years now. Lincoln Avenue   *
          and West 24th Street.   *

                    CLARK   *
          Oh. And what color is the car?   *

                    RICHARD   *
          Grey. Clark, what are you going   *
          to do, mount an aerial search?   *
               (types on computer)
          Damn.

                    CLARK
          What?

                    RICHARD
          She has a password.

Richard tries different things: *Jason, Richard, etc*... but
nothing works. Clark reluctantly sighs.

                    CLARK
          Try 'Superman'.

Richard types it in. The computer unlocks, just as ZAP! THE
POWER GOES OUT.

214   **EXT. EARTH FROM SPACE – SAME TIME**   214

The Earth rotates as the blackout spreads across the
planet... when the lights suddenly COME BACK ON.

214A   **INT. DAILY PLANET - BULLPEN - LOIS' DESK**   214A

The Daily Planet lights come back on. Everyone breathes a
sigh of relief. Everyone but Clark.

215   **INT. YACHT - MAIN ROOM**   215

Lois looks up as the power is restored -- and the fax
machine starts up again.

216   **EXT. UNDER THE OCEAN**   216

As the crystal plunges deeper into the dark waters, the
glow within the rocket's compartment intensifies.

CLOSE ON THE CRYSTAL: it begins to GROW. NEW BRANCHES
appear on its surface, MELDING with the kryptonite. BOOM!
The crystal grows so large that it SHATTERS the rocket,
then continues on its descent.

Approaching the ocean floor, the crystal disappears into a
DEEP CHASM, and a BLAST OF LIGHT illuminates the sea for
miles.

217   **EXT. YACHT - DECK**   217

Everyone averts their eyes. Lex seems to bask in the light.

218   **INT. YACHT - MAIN ROOM**   218

THE LIGHT blasts through the glass-bottom, filling the
room. Startled, Brutus stands up just as the light fades.
Beat. Lois nervously waits to see what he'll do. Suddenly,
Jason starts playing the piano again. Brutus looks at Lois,
then at Jason, then sits back down and plays again.

219   **EXT. YACHT - DECK - CONTINUOUS**   219

BOOM! THUNDER CRACKS. Lightning flashes. Kitty and Lex look
up at thick, rumbling clouds overhead. It's beginning.

                         KITTY
              Lex, this isn't like the train
              set.

                         LEX
                    (confident)
              I know.

220   **INT. OCEAN FLOOR - SAME TIME**   220

BOOM! A FLASH OF LIGHT and a SEA OF BUBBLES, as HUGE CRACKS
FORM ALONG THE OCEAN FLOOR, spreading for miles. They grow
deeper, turning into vast chasms. The ground RUMBLES, and
MASSIVE CRYSTAL COLUMNS begin to rise out of the chasms.

224A   **INT. YACHT - MAIN ROOM - SAME TIME**   224A

Brutus and Jason are still playing a bad duet on the piano, so Lois takes the opportunity and hits REDIAL on the fax machine. It CONNECTS and starts to send. The paper moves through the machine -- past 'HELP US' -- past the coordinates -- and just as Lois' name is about to go through...

THE POWER DIES AGAIN. But only the fax machine seems to be affected. Then Lois looks up to see BRUTUS, holding the power cord, pissed. Lois smiles. BRUTUS GRABS HER and throws her across the room, SLAMMING her against a bannister. Jason stops playing, watching as Brutus storms towards her.

225   **INT. DAILY PLANET - BULLPEN**   225

THE FAX MACHINE BEEPS and spits out Lois' message: *HELP US!*   *
40N73W -- but the rest is cut off. Gil picks it up. Not   *
realizing who it's from, he just looks at the message,   *
perplexed.   *

Meanwhile, JIMMY sits at his desk, idly taking photos of   *
other staff members.   *

CAMERA LENS POV: A woman on the phone. Perry pacing in his   *
office. Richard and Clark at Lois' desk. POV drifts to GIL   *
holding Lois' fax. Zooms in.   *

Jimmy sees the message. Alarmed, he gets up.   *

226   **INT. DAILY PLANET - LOIS' DESK - MOMENTS LATER**   226

Jimmy slams the fax down in front of Richard and Clark. They both grab it at the same time, almost as if fighting for it.

                    RICHARD
          Where did you get this?

                    JIMMY
          It came through the fax. It's
          Lois' handwriting -- I'd
          recognize it anywhere, but I
          don't know what it means...

          RICHARD   CLARK
     They're coordinates.   They're coordinates.

Beat. Richard and Clark exchange glances.

                    RICHARD
          Twenty miles off the coast.
          Jimmy, call the Coast Guard and
          tell Perry that I'm taking the
          sea plane.

Richard starts to leave, then stops.

                        RICHARD (CONT'D)
          Clark?

Clark stares at the numbers, then at Richard, thinking.

                        CLARK
          No thanks. I'm not feeling very   *
          well.   *

Richard nods and leaves. Clark watches until he's gone.
Then:

                        CLARK (CONT'D)   *
          Jimmy, I'm going to get some air.   *

227   **INT. DAILY PLANET - ELEVATOR BANK - MOMENTS LATER**   227

Clark steps into an elevator. The doors shut.

228   **INT. ELEVATOR - CONTINUOUS**   228

THE SHIRT is ripped open, revealing SUPERMAN'S CREST. In
one swift movement, Clark's clothes seem to fall from his
body as he rises up through the elevator hatch...

229   **OMITTED**   229

230   **INT. ELEVATOR SHAFT - SAME TIME**   230

VWOOSH! SUPERMAN flies straight up the elevator shaft.

231   **EXT. DAILY PLANET - ROOFTOP - MOMENTS LATER**   231

...BLASTING OUT OF THE ROOFTOP DOOR and into the sky.

232   **EXT. SKY - MOMENTS LATER**   232

Superman soars out of the city and over the water, racing
to reach Lois. Suddenly, he hears strange sounds building
in the sea below: A RUMBLING, followed by a deep CRACKING
SOUND. Alarmed, he stops and looks down at the water.

X-RAY POV: Through the water, he sees the ocean floor just
as it RUPTURES, releasing BLACK DUST from the sea-floor,
shifting the ground like it's on a FAULT LINE. The rupture
continues, travelling along the ocean floor, past Superman.

Superman looks up, and realizes it's headed straight for
METROPOLIS. Beat. He turns and stares at the horizon,
thinking of Lois. Torn.

236   **INT. YACHT - MAIN ROOM**   236   *

Lois darts to the POOL TABLE with Brutus right on her   *
heels. She grabs a POOL CUE and swings, SMASHING it against   *
him. Once. Twice. On the third swipe, he CATCHES it with   *
one hand, and grabs HER NECK with the other. Brutus   *
squeezes, choking her, then hurls her against the wall and   *
into a shelf. Lois collapses to the ground, barely   *
conscious. He stands over her, ready to STRIKE HER WITH THE   *
POOL CUE, when   *

THE ENTIRE PIANO COMES FLYING TOWARDS HIM. SMASH! It   *
collides and shatters. Broken piano keys scatter across the   *
floor.   *

Lois looks up to see JASON standing with arms outstretched,   *
paralyzed with fear. *Did I just do that?*   *

He takes a hit off his inhaler, then rushes to his mother,   *
terrified. She's just as shaken, trying to calm both Jason   *
and herself down.   *

                    LOIS   *
          It's... okay.   *

She painfully stands and takes him by the hand. They start   *
to make their way to the stairs when RILEY AND GRANT come   *
down the spiral staircase. They see Brutus' feet poking out   *
from under the piano, and stare at Lois and Jason, stunned.   *

237   **INT. YACHT - PANTRY - MOMENTS LATER**   237

The men toss Lois and Jason into a long, narrow pantry.
WHAM! The door is slammed. Locked. Lois ferociously pounds
on it.

                    LOIS (BEHIND DOOR)
          OPEN THIS DOOR! OPEN IT!

She turns to Jason -- as if looking for help. But he just   *
puts his arms around her and hugs her tightly.   *

238-240A **OMITTED**   238-240A

240B **INT. YACHT - BRIDGE - SAME TIME**   240B

The ship is rocking back and forth. Kitty tries to keep her
balance, clearly not having a good time.

Lex stares at the SONAR SCREEN, which displays strange
structures forming in the ocean. Riley and Grant enter.

                    GRANT
          We had a little problem
          downstairs. Brutus got hit with   *
          the... *piano.*   *

A look of dread washes over Lex's face.   *

                    LEX
          Where's the boy?   *

                    GRANT
          Locked up with his mother. In the   *
          pantry.

Beat. Lex thinks about that for a moment, obviously
bothered. He looks down at THE SONAR IMAGE-- the structures
are getting larger.

                    LEX
          Get the helicopter ready.

Lex walks to the counter where Stanford dismantled the
missile, opens up A DRAWER, and removes a MONOGRAMMED
HANDKERCHIEF from his coat pocket...

241   **INT. YACHT - MAIN CABIN - MOMENTS LATER**   241

Lex descends the spiral staircase and walks toward his desk, stunned by what he sees:

THE SHATTERED PIANO with Brutus still underneath. We only   *
see his legs poking out from the debris.

Realizing what happened, Lex quickly scoops up the
Kryptonian crystals and leaves.   *

242   **INT. YACHT - PANTRY**   242

Lois and Jason sit against the far wall, exhausted and worried.

CLICK. She hears the door unlocking. Sees the knob turn. It swings open, revealing LEX. He looks at Jason and winks.

                    LEX
          Catch.

He tosses SOMETHING into the room, wrapped in the handkerchief. It smashes to the floor, rolling towards Jason's feet. LOIS CHARGES just as Lex slams the door shut again.

Lois turns and looks at Jason. The boy removes Lex's handkerchief, revealing THE EXPLOSIVE taken from the missile.

Her eyes widen in horror.

                    LOIS
          Honey... don't move.

243   **EXT. YACHT - HELIPAD - MOMENTS LATER**   243

Blades spin. The helicopter lifts off with Lex and his crew safely inside.

245   **OMITTED**   245

245A   **EXT. UNDERWATER - MOMENTS LATER**   245A

Deep underwater, the rupture moves faster, racing hundreds
of miles an hour into shallower water. As it approaches the
SHORELINE, it gets absorbed in the ground and SPREADS
OUTWARDS.

CAMERA MOVES UP and out of the water, revealing the
METROPOLIS SKYLINE.

245B   **OMITTED**   245B

245C   **OMITTED**   245C

245D   **OMITTED**   245D

246   **EXT. METROPOLIS STREET - MOMENTS LATER**   246

Peopling are going about their daily routine. A FAINT
RUMBLE starts to build. Windows rattle. A MOTHER pulls her
SON close.   *

251   **INT. DAILY PLANET - PERRY'S OFFICE - SAME TIME**   251

Perry is staring at Lois' fax.

                    PERRY
          What are these, lottery numbers?

The LIGHTS flicker.

                    PERRY (CONT'D)
          Christ, not another blackout.

Jimmy hears a CAR ALARM outside. It seems unremarkable,
until he hears another, and another. They become a chorus
of alarms. Then, a DEEP RUMBLE. Awards on Perry's wall
SHAKE.

                    JIMMY
          I don't think it's just another
          blackout.

Perry feels it. He gets up from his desk and slowly walks
to the doorway. He can see the staff nervously looking
around, feeling the faint rumble.

Meanwhile, Jimmy stares out at the Metropolis skyline. IN
THE DISTANCE, he sees skyscraper windows shattering and
pieces of debris falling, and this disturbance seems to be
moving through the city like a wave -- TOWARDS THEM. Jimmy
is stunned, barely able to speak.

                    JIMMY (CONT'D)
               (quietly)
          Chief...?

251A   **EXT. BULLPEN - LOIS'S DESK**   251A

The rumbling knocks LOIS' FAMILY PHOTO off of her desk. It shatters on the floor.

SMASH CUT TO:

251B   **EXT. METROPOLIS OVERHEAD**   251B

FROM ABOVE, we move over Metropolis and see what can only be described as A SHOCKWAVE ripping through the entire city. GAS MAINS and ELECTRICAL FIRES spark and explode.   ★
It's chaos.   ★

251C   **OMITTED**   251C   ★

251D   **EXT. DAILY PLANET - SAME TIME**   251D   ★

The shockwave travels up the building, SHATTERING WINDOWS, hitting the RAM'S HEADS on its way towards the roof...

251Dpt2 **INT. DAILY PLANET - BULLPEN - SAME TIME**   251Dpt2

THE SHOCKWAVE tears through the room, starting with Perry's office and rippling across the bullpen.

THE ENTIRE FLOOR seems to rise and fall like a wave. MONITORS spark and explode. Overhead lights and windows shatter. Staff are knocked to their feet.

...then it suddenly STOPS.

251E   **EXT. DAILY PLANET - ROOFTOP - SAME TIME**   251E

THE DAILY PLANET GLOBE is hit. The base cracks.

251F-G   **OMITTED**   251F-G

251J   **INT. DAILY PLANET - BULLPEN**   251J

The SHOCKWAVE is over as quickly as it began. Beat. Perry looks out over the stunned bullpen.

> PERRY
> Okay, everyone stay put and stay
> calm!

JIMMY notices one of the RAM'S HEADS starting to CRACK.

> JIMMY
> Um... Chief?

> PERRY
> Olsen, don't call me...

PERRY TURNS just in time to see the RAM'S HEAD break off and fall from his balcony.

                        PERRY (CONT'D)
                   (back to the bullpen)
              OKAY, EVERYONE OUT! NICE AND
              ORDERLY -- DOWN THE STAIRS! MOVE!

251K-M **OMITTED**   251K-M

252   **EXT. METROPOLIS - DAY**   252

    THE SHOCKWAVE as it hits A SKYSCRAPER, shattering all of   *
the BROKEN GLASS and other debris cascades
down toward people on the crowded street.   *

    Suddenly, SUPERMAN swoops down from the sky. FLYING ON HIS   *
BACK directly under the falling debris.   *

    CLOSE ON: his eyes -- GLOWING, building with power. The air   *
begins to RIPPLE. It grows in intensity, coalescing into a   *
POWERFUL RAY OF HEAT VISION THAT BLASTS FROM HIS EYES.   *

    THE HEAT VISION creates a light as bright as the sun, and   *
VWAP! ENGULFS the falling debris.   *

    PEOPLE ON THE STREET gawk upward, watching as the shower of
glass and metal instantly become harmless bits of ash and
ember. It's almost beautiful. VWOOSH! Superman rockets   *
through the glowing embers and continues onward.

    WITHOUT STOPPING: Superman catches a falling CONSTRUCTION   *
WORKER and safely sets him on a rooftop.   *

    A BILLBOARD tumbles towards the street but with a single   *
punch, Superman knocks it aside.   *

    CAMERA DROPS TO THREE PEOPLE trying to pull a young man
from a burning, overturned car. Suddenly, a blurry streak   *
whips by and VWOOSH -the fire is extinguished -- leaving   *
the car covered in a thin layer of frost.   *

    A FIFTEEN FOOT GEYSER OF FLAME gushes from a cracked GAS   *
MAIN. VWOOSH! Superman rockets past and effortlessly blows   *
it out like a candle, just as he flies towards--   *

    ANOTHER FIRE engulfing an apartment building, where A DOZEN   *
PEOPLE are trapped on the roof. VWOOOOOOSH! Superman   *
focuses his breath, concentrating it on the blaze. His   *
superbreath fills the building, and after a moment -- the   *
fire is gone.   *

    Superman sighs, finally taking a breather, when he suddenly   *
JOLTS -- HEARING something in the deep distance -- a CRACK.

253   **EXT. DAILY PLANET - ROOFTOP - SAME TIME**   253

CRACK! The base of the DAILY PLANET GLOBE shatters
completely. SPARKS FLY. The globe teeters back and forth,
then BREAKS OFF. It crashes onto the rooftop, SMASHING into
the water tower...

253A   **EXT. APARTMENT BUILDING - SAME TIME**   253A   *

Realizing what's happening, Superman flies back towards the
Daily Planet.   *

254   **EXT. DAILY PLANET - PLAZA**   254

SNAP! SNAP! SNAP! Jimmy takes photos of the staff streaming
out of the building, nearly tripping over THE BROKEN RAM'S
HEAD embedded in the pavement.

PERRY feels water from above. Is it rain? Confused, he
looks up, just in time to see THE GLOBE rolling off the
edge.

                        PERRY
                  (quietly to himself)
               Great Caesar's ghost.

255   **EXT. DAILY PLANET - CONTINUOUS**   255

The globe scrapes the side of the building.

255A   **EXT. METROPOLIS STREETS - SAME TIME**   255A

Superman rockets over crowded streets, faster than we've
ever seen him move.

SUPERMAN'S POV: winding around buildings and intersections
like they're trees. His POV speeds up and BEELINES STRAIGHT
TOWARDS A BUILDING.

255B   **EXT. DAILY PLANET - PLAZA**   255B

PEOPLE SCREAM AND SCATTER.

255C   **EXT. STREETS - SAME TIME**   255C

Superman blasts towards the Daily Planet, and WITHOUT
STOPPING, flies through a window...

255D   **INT. DAILY PLANET - OFFICE- CONTINUOUS**   255D

...continuing THROUGH an empty office, then THROUGH A
WALL...

255E   **EXT. DAILY PLANET - PLAZA - CONTINUOUS**   255E

The giant globe is seconds from crushing the crowd.

Jimmy looks up and SNAP! SNAP! SNAP! takes MORE PHOTOS: THE GLOBE a hundred feet above -- fifty feet -- twenty -- then...

SUPERMAN exploding out of the Daily Planet and SWOOPING UNDER THE GLOBE, catching it in the nick of time.

HE LOWERS IT DOWN on his shoulders like ATLAS, then sets it on top of a car.

Jimmy lowers his camera, realizing he just got THE PERFECT PHOTOGRAPH.

People clear out of the way. Superman steps back, resting. He's exhausted. The crowd stares at him, awestruck.

Then as mysteriously as the quake started, it quiets and stops. Perry emerges from the crowd.

                    PERRY
          Superman! Perry White, Daily
          Planet. What the hell just
          happened!?

Before he can answer, SUPERMAN HEARS something in the distance -- A MASSIVE UNEARTHLY RUMBLING -- the sound of something much larger approaching. He realizes this isn't over.

                    SUPERMAN
          I'm not sure, but I'm going to
          find out.

Perry digests the information and just nods. Superman turns to leave, when Perry remembers...

                    PERRY
          Wait! Lois is missing.

                    SUPERMAN
          I know.

WHOOSH! He takes off.

256   **INT. YACHT - MAIN ROOM - SAME TIME**   256

    Camera creeps along the floor, past the piano. Through the   *
    glass bottom: it's dark and murky, but then huge GLEAMING
    WHITE CRYSTALS appear, snaking through the water.

256A   **EXT. UNDERWATER - SAME TIME**   256A

    As the central structure expands, it grows outward -- and
    massive CRYSTALS emerge from the ground, following the
    INITIAL RUPTURE LINE...

    ...HEADING STRAIGHT FOR THE COASTLINE... AND METROPOLIS.

257   **INT. LEX'S HELICOPTER**   257

    Lex stares out the window, at a field of giant crystals
    rising from the water below.

258   **EXT. OCEAN - SAME TIME**   258

    In the distance, a crystal SUPERSTRUCTURE breaks the
    surface.

259-260 **OMITTED**   259-260

260A   **INT. YACHT - PANTRY**   260A

    Lois is panicked, searching for a window, a porthole, any
    possible way to get rid of the explosive. Finally, she
    spots A SMALL AIR DUCT near the floor. She kneels down and
    pulls at the VENT COVER. It won't budge. She looks around,
    looking for a tool, and sees a LARGE METALLIC SOUP LADLE
    hanging on the wall.

    SHE JAMS THE LADLE INTO THE VENT, using it like a crowbar.
    Jason senses her fear and steps towards her--

                    JASON
      Mommy?

                    LOIS
         JASON, DON'T MOVE!

    Lois strains to pry the vent away. After what seems like an
    eternity, it finally pops off. She then approaches Jason
    VERY CAREFULLY.

                  LOIS (CONT'D)
        Okay honey, stay still...

    Lois nervously takes the explosive from his hands, carries
    it to the vent, and THROWS IT into the air duct. She
    immediately grabs Jason and rushes him to the other side of
    the room, shielding him from the possible explosion.

    CLANG! CLUNK! CLANG! They hear the explosive drop down a
    series of air ducts. The noise gradually fades as it falls
    farther and farther away. Silence. Beat.

Lois and Jason open their eyes. She lets out a heavy sigh, Relieved. Then -- BOOOOOOOOOOM!

260B   **EXT. UNDERWATER - SAME TIME**   260B

FROM BELOW, we see the hull EXPLODE outward, creating a gaping hole.

261   **INT. YACHT - PANTRY - SAME TIME**   261   *

THE BLAST ROCKS THE ROOM. A burst of flame shoots from the   *
vent. Lois shields Jason. The flames subside, but are   *
quickly followed by a GEYSER OF SEAWATER.   *

262   **EXT. YACHT - SAME TIME**   262

The ship is half-submerged and sinking fast. ZAP! The   *
lights go out.

263   **INT. YACHT - PANTRY**   263

Half of the room is tipped upward. Water is streaming in.
Lois tumbles backwards into the water, struggling to reach
Jason, who is clutching to a shelf, but she's STUCK.

ANGLE UNDERWATER: Lois's leg, ironically tangled in the
ropes of a LIFE PRESERVER.

                    LOIS
          HELP ME! Oh God...

Jason starts to hyperventilate. HE'S HAVING AN ASTHMA
ATTACK, but can't find his inhaler. He stares in horror as
Lois fights to stay above water, screaming:

                    LOIS (CONT'D)
          HELP!

Water floods into her mouth. She disappears under the
surface when the DOOR is suddenly RIPPED OPEN, AND THE
SILHOUETTE OF A MAN STEPS INTO THE ROOM. He dives
underwater.

UNDERWATER: The man rips Lois' leg free from the cables.

ABOVE WATER: He pulls her to safety -- to the dry side of
the room. Lois finally opens her eyes and comes face to
face with... RICHARD. She and Jason are both stunned.

                    LOIS (CONT'D)
          How -- How did you get here?

                    RICHARD
               (obviously...)
          I flew.

264   **EXT. OCEAN SURFACE - SAME TIME**   264

RICHARD'S SEA PLANE rests on the water nearby.

We hear a RUMBLE. The water under the yacht begins to churn
and BUBBLE, like something is about to break the surface...

265   **INT. YACHT - PANTRY - MOMENTS LATER**   265

They start heading for the DOORWAY.   *

                        RICHARD
                Lois, what have you gotten
                yourself into?

                        LOIS
                Don't blame me! This is Lex
                Luthor's mess.

They hear a metallic GROAN and feel THE SHIP lurching.

                        RICHARD
                What is that...

                        LOIS
                GRAB ONTO SOMETHING!

265A   **EXT. OCEAN SURFACE - SAME TIME**   265A

A HUGE CRYSTAL COLUMN rises out of the water. It hits the
bottom of the yacht, PIERCING THE HULL.

265B   **INT. YACHT - MAIN ROOM**   265B

THE CRYSTAL shatters the glass bottom, rising to the
ceiling.

265C   **INT. YACHT - PANTRY**   265C *

Lois, Jason, and Richard cling to each other while the   *
entire pantry tips upwards.   *

266   **EXT. OCEAN SURFACE - SAME TIME**   266

THE CRYSTAL HAS PIERCED THE MIDDLE OF THE YACHT, lifting it
out of the water, before finally BREAKING IT IN HALF.

THE FRONT PORTION of the ship breaks away and falls into
the water, sinking quickly.

THE REAR HALF crashes back down into the water, barely
afloat. Water bubbles. It too starts sinking. The different
levels of the ship are visible, as is THE PANTRY IN WHICH   *
LOIS, RICHARD AND JASON ARE TRAPPED.

267   **INT. YACHT - PANTRY - CONTINUOUS**   267 *

The pantry is tipping backwards. Seawater rushes in.   *

LOIS SEES THE SKY through the open doorway. She can also   *
see that THE DOOR is ABOUT TO SLAM SHUT. She climbs towards *
it.   *

                           LOIS
              NO!!!

                         RICHARD
              Lois, wait!

WHAM! THE DOOR slams shut against her head. She tumbles
back, landing unconscious next to Richard and Jason.

                      RICHARD (CONT'D)
              Lois!!!

Richard grabs her with one arm and holds Jason with the
other. WATER IS POURING IN ALL AROUND THEM, filling the
room.

268A   **EXT. UNDERWATER - SAME TIME**   268A

        The broken hull sinks into the ocean, joining other chunks
        of debris from the yacht. The only sign of life is the beam
        of Richard's flashlight shining through the porthole.

268B   **INT. YACHT - PANTRY - SAME TIME**   268B

        Water has filled the room to the ceiling. Richard holds
        Jason and Lois close. It seems hopeless. Just then: BOOM!
        TWO RED BOOTS LAND ON THE OTHER SIDE OF THE PORTHOLE.   *

268BA   **EXT. UNDERWATER - SAME TIME**   268BA   *

        Superman grabs hold of the ship with his right hand...   *

268C   **EXT. WATER SURFACE - CONTINUOUS**   268C   *

        ...and easily pulls the hull to the ocean surface with   *
        everyone still inside.   *

268D   **INT. YACHT - PANTRY**   268D   *

        Murky water gives way to clouds. The door opens. Richard   *
        gawks up at Superman, who extends his left hand.   *

                         SUPERMAN   *
              Here, take my hand!   *

        Richard makes sure he has a hold of Jason and Lois, then   *
        grabs Superman's arm.   *

                         RICHARD   *
              Got us?   *

                         SUPERMAN   *
              Got you.   *

269   **EXT. WATER SURFACE - CONTINUOUS**   269   *

        ...and with that, Superman releases, letting the broken   *
        hull sink back into the ocean.   *

270   **EXT. SEA PLANE - MOMENTS LATER**   270

Superman gently lands them onto the pontoons. Richard sets
Jason down. Superman is still cradling Lois. Beat.
Realizing he's holding onto her a bit too long, he lays her
down.

USING HIS X-RAY VISION, Superman looks her over. Richard
stares at the Man of Steel, dumbfounded and panicked.

                    RICHARD
          You... you're-- him.

                    SUPERMAN
              (still focused on Lois)
          You must be Richard. I've heard
          so much about you.

270   **EXT. SEA PLANE - MOMENTS LATER**   270

Superman gently lands them onto the pontoons. Richard sets
Jason down. Superman is still cradling Lois. Beat.
Realizing he's holding onto her a bit too long, he lays her
down.

USING HIS X-RAY VISION, Superman looks her over. Richard
stares at the Man of Steel, dumbfounded and panicked.   *

                    SUPERMAN
              She'll be fine.

BOOM! A BLAST OF WIND HITS THEM. THE WATER RAGES. Crystal
columns are emerging everywhere. They stare, awestruck.   *

Jason curiously looks up at Superman.

                    JASON
              Hey, you look just like--

                    SUPERMAN
                 (cutting him off)
              Can you fly?

For a moment, it looks like Superman is speaking to Jason --   *
then he turns his head to Richard.   *

                    RICHARD
              What?

                    SUPERMAN
              Can you fly out of here?

                    RICHARD
              I can't take off in this.

                    SUPERMAN
              Alright, I'll point you in the   *
              right direction. Just promise me   *
              you won't come back.   *

                    RICHARD
              I promise.
                 (beat)   *
              Hey!   *

Superman stops on his way out.   *

                    RICHARD (CONT'D)   *
              Thank you.   *

271   **EXT. NEW KRYPTON - MOMENTS LATER**   271

The seaplane safely soars away.

CAMERA DROPS DOWN TO Superman, soaring over the landscape.
It's eerily familiar, almost identical to the remains of
Krypton.

Confused and awestruck, he swoops towards the center of the
structure. It too is familiar. It's the size of an arena,
with CRYSTAL MONOLITHS arranged in a circle. In the center,
rests a structure resembling the FORTRESS OF SOLITUDE. Next
to it is LEX'S HELICOPTER. Empty.

272   **EXT. NEW KRYPTON - VALLEY OF ELDERS - CONTINUOUS**   272

BOOM. Superman lands hard, staring upward. This place is
also familiar. It's an exact reproduction of the Kryptonian
VALLEY OF ELDERS. Only the family crests are missing.

But unlike the ruins, this place feels like it could be
full of life -- what he hoped to find when he went to
Krypton. A ghostly wind makes it even more unnerving. Then,
Superman hears something else in the wind, coming from
inside the structure: a VOICE. Faint, but familiar. Maybe
JOR-EL? LARA? It's joined by other ghostly whispers before
another familiar voice calls out:

                    LEX (O.S.)
          See anything familiar?

REVEAL: Lex standing at the top of a staircase that leads
to a new fortress. Kitty is with him.

                    SUPERMAN
          I see an old man's sick joke.

Superman ascends the stairs and sees Riley's camcorder
focused on him. Annoyed, he focuses and MELTS THE CAMERA
WITH HIS HEAT VISION. But something is wrong. Superman
realizes his powers are somehow *weaker*. He's beginning to
sweat. Lex notices.

                    LEX
          Really? Because I see my new
          apartment. And a space for Kitty,
          and my friends, and that one
          there I'll rent out.
                    (beat)
          No, you're right. It is a little
          cold. A little... alien. It needs
          that human touch.

Superman and Lex stare at each other. Face to face.

                    SUPERMAN
          I don't have time for this,
          Luthor. You have something that
          belongs to me.

Superman starts to pass him when LEX PUNCHES HIM ACROSS THE FACE. WHAM! The Man of Steel falls, reeling in PAIN.

273   **INT. SEA PLANE - SAME TIME**   273

Richard is at the controls. Lois lays in a seat next to Jason. He caresses her gently.

>   JASON
>   Wake up, mommy. Wake up...

HER EYES SPRING OPEN. She gasps, looks around, startled.

>   RICHARD
>   Hey. It's alright. We're safe.

Lois looks out the window, realizes they're flying.

>   LOIS
>   How...

>   RICHARD
>   Superman.

>   LOIS
>   Where is he?!

>   RICHARD
>   He went back to stop Luthor.

Lois' eyes widen in horror, remembering the kryptonite.

>   LOIS
>   Richard, we have to turn around.

>   RICHARD
>   What?!

>   LOIS
>   Turn the plane around. Please.

Richard looks at her, then at Jason. Jason nods in agreement -- and a decision is made between the three of them.

274   **EXT. NEW KRYPTON - VALLEY OF ELDERS**   274

>   LEX
>   Kryptonite. You're asking
>   yourself "how?".
>   (looks around)
>   Didn't your dad ever tell you to
>   look before you leap?

Superman focuses, and using his x-ray vision, sees what Lex is talking about.

X-RAY VISION POV: IN THE GROUND AND WALLS are pockets and
veins of kryptonite, growths that occurred when the crystal
grew through the kryptonite shard.

> LEX (CONT'D)
> Crystals are amazing aren't they?

WHAM! Lex kicks him.

> LEX (CONT'D)
> They inherit the traits of the
> minerals around them.

WHAM! Lex kicks him again.

> LEX (CONT'D)
> Sort of like a son inheriting the
> traits of his father.

WHAM!

> LEX (CONT'D)
> Look buddy, we sent you there to
> die, but ya' had to come back...

Superman looks at Lex, his expression turning from agony to
realization.

> LEX (CONT'D)
> Oh yeah. All those photos? Those
> stories about Krypton still
> existing? It was me.
> (beat)
> And him.

ANGLE ON: Stanford.

> LEX (CONT'D)
> Thankfully the press doesn't
> check facts like they used to.
> (beat)
> Hey, you took away five years of
> my life. I just returned the
> favor.

Lex tries to kick him again, but Superman GRABS HIS ANKLE
and twists it, about to yank him to the ground.

Suddenly, RILEY grabs Superman and PICKS HIM UP and hurls
him against a wall, shattering crystal outgrowths. Lex's
men surround the fallen hero like a pack of hungry wolves.

GRANT delivers a swift punch to his jaw. Superman lunges, struggling to fight back, but it's futile, and they proceed to beat him like a normal man.

Kitty flinches, covers her eyes. It's brutal.

As Superman crawls to the edge of a steep cliff, LEX reaches into his pocket, and pulls out THE KRYPTONITE SHARD chipped from the meteorite.

FROM OVERHEAD, we see the drop is steep, almost endless. Superman peers over the edge. He suddenly SCREAMS IN PAIN, ARCHING BACKWARDS.

BEHIND SUPERMAN

Lex has stabbed the kryptonite shard deep into Superman's back. CRACK! Lex breaks the shard off, leaving most of it inside the wound. A strange pulse of green light flows into Superman's body.

>   LEX (CONT'D)
>   (whispers)
>   Now, fly.

Lex steps back, watching Superman die.

Superman looks down the cliffside behind him. This is the moment. Then -- HE LEAPS OFF THE EDGE.

275   **EXT. NEW KRYPTON - CLIFFSIDE - CONTINUOUS**   275

He tumbles head over heel, dropping hundreds of feet.

276   **EXT. NEW KRYPTON - VALLEY OF ELDERS**   276

Lex stands at the edge of the cliff, staring down.

277   **EXT. UNDERWATER - CONTINUOUS**   277

SPLASH! Superman plunges into the water, sinking deep. Tumbling and spinning, Superman opens his eyes, disoriented. Crystals are growing towards him from every direction. Smaller shards float in the water, All GLOWING GREEN from Kryptonite. He tries swimming to the surface, but he's too weak. He's trapped.

ANGLE ON: the shard embedded in his back. He tries to reach it, but can't.

He opens his mouth in a silent scream. He's struggling to stay alive. A mesh of crystal walls are closing in around him, over him. It's like a tomb.

279   **INT. SEA PLANE - SAME TIME**   279

Richard pilots towards the massive growing continent, when Jason looks out the window, pointing down at the water.

                    JASON
          There.

He turns to Lois. Beat. She can't see anything.

                    LOIS
          You're sure?

Jason nods. He's certain.   *

280   **EXT. UNDERWATER - SAME TIME**   280

      ONE LAST BUBBLE escapes from Superman's mouth. He stops
      moving. Lifeless. Sinking. Disappearing into the darkness.

      Suddenly -- VWOOSH -- from above, we hear the sound of
      something approaching and see the PONTOONS of the seaplane   *
      tear across the surface of the water.   *

280A **INT. SEA PLANE - MOMENTS LATER**   280A *

      The plane stops. Richard removes his seatbelt when he turns *
      to see Lois THROW THE DOOR OPEN.   *

                    RICHARD   *
          What are you doing?!   *

She jumps into the water.   *

280B **EXT. UNDERWATER - SAME TIME**   280B *

      CLOSE ON: SUPERMAN'S HAND, listlessly reaching upwards as   *
      if trying to grab hold of something. It slowly sinks,
      descending out of frame, his RED CAPE trailing behind.
      Suddenly--

      ANOTHER HAND GRABS THE CAPE and pulls it tight.   *

281   **EXT. SEA PLANE - CONTINUOUS**   281

      The plane rests on the surface. Richard and Jason anxiously
      stare at the water. Beat. LOIS SURFACES, gasping for air.
      She has Superman wrapped in her arms. Richard rushes to   *
      help.   *

283   **INT. SEA PLANE - SAME TIME**   283

      Lois cradles Superman. She slaps him, trying to wake him
      up, His eyes are rolled back. *He's dying.*

                    LOIS
          Wake up! Come on! Wake up!

RICHARD is at the controls, desperately trying to get the
plane in the air.

284   **EXT. NEW KRYPTON - CANYON**   284

The plane cruises through the choppy water, but can't seem
to lift off. It swerves, barely dodging more crystal
structures rising out of the water.

285   **INT. SEA PLANE - SAME TIME**   285

Superman slowly starts to awaken, rambling...

                    SUPERMAN
            Kryptonite... there's Kryptonite
            in the crystals.

                     LOIS
       We have to get him away from
       here!

                     RICHARD
       I'm trying! The water's too
       choppy and *he's* too heavy.

Through the window, Richard sees the crystals in front of
them are closing in fast -- but there's still room to make
it through. His eyes widen.

                  RICHARD (CONT'D)
     SEAT BELTS!

Jason straps in.

286   **EXT. NEW KRYPTON - CANYON**   286

The plane makes it just between the crystals but then we
realize they're at the top of a giant WATERFALL -- the
structure has risen a thousand feet higher.

They PLUMMET straight downward towards the OCEAN...

...but just before the plane hits the water below, IT
CATCHES THE AIR AND PULLS UP, safely soaring into the sky.

287   **INT. SEA PLANE**   287

Feeling something in Superman's back, Lois pulls his cape   *
away, REVEALING: THE STAB WOUND. She can see the broken   *
shard still embedded near his spine. Horrified, she looks   *
for something to pull it out with.   *

                     LOIS   *
       Richard, I need pliers!   *

                     RICHARD   *
       There's a toolbox under the seat!   *

She spots the toolbox and fumbles it open. Various tools   *
spill over the floor, including a pair of NEEDLE-NOSE   *
PLIERS.   *

Lois nervously stares at the wound, then inserts the   *
pliers, trying to get a grasp on the shard. It's not easy. *
Finally, she feels it, and pulls the pliers out-- revealing *
the kryptonite. There is no blood --- it's more like a   *
burn. Lois opens the door and throws the kryptonite from   *
the plane.   *

288   **EXT. SKY - SAME TIME**   288

WE FOLLOW the shard from the sky until it finally splashes
into the water below.

288A **EXT. METROPOLIS COAST – SAME TIME**   288A

A gathering crowd stares at the horizon. They can see STORM
CLOUDS in the distance, spreading towards them.

288B **OMITTED**   288B *

289 **INT. SEA PLANE – SAME TIME**   289 *

Superman opens his eyes to see everyone staring. He's weak,
but regaining his strength.

                    SUPERMAN
          How did you find me?

                    LOIS
          You're hurt.

                    SUPERMAN
          I'll be alright.
               (to Richard)
                    (MORE)

                              SUPERMAN (CONT'D)
                    You promised you wouldn't come
                    back. You lied.

                              RICHARD
                    I'm not you. I can do that.

Superman OPENS THE DOOR. WIND pours into the plane.

                              SUPERMAN
                    I have to go back.

                              LOIS
                    No! You'll die if you go back!

They lock eyes. Longing. Uncertain. Frightened.

                              SUPERMAN
                    Goodbye, Lois.

And with that, Superman leans back, and VWOOSH-- he's gone.

290   **EXT. SKY - CONTINUOUS**   290

      FROM OVERHEAD, he fully sees the extent of the damage. New
      Krypton is huge and still expanding.

      Superman flies high into the air, through the storm clouds,
      entering the stratosphere.

291   **EXT. SPACE - CONTINUOUS**   291

      WARM SUNLIGHT washes over him. He almost seems to bask in
      it for a moment, as if regaining his strength. The Earth is
      far below. Then, he arches backward and DIVES STRAIGHT
      DOWN.

      Superman re-enters the atmosphere with such speed and power
      that the air around him IGNITES, glowing brightly. He
      continues diving downward, and as he does, A RIPPLE OF HEAT
      VISION blasts from his eyes...

292   **EXT. SKY - CONTINUOUS**   292

      ...and vaporizes A CLOUD BANK. VWOOSH! Superman soars
      through -- A second later, his HEAT VISION hits...

292A **EXT. OCEAN SURFACE - CONTINUOUS**   292A

      ...the ocean surface. It starts to BUBBLE and MIST just as
      he plunges into the sea.

293   **EXT. UNDER THE OCEAN - CONTINUOUS**   293

      He travels the speed of sound through the murky water,
      towards the ocean floor. Using his heat vision to melt the
      rocky earth into liquid magma, he blasts into the ground,
      disappearing.

A huge cloud of sand and dirt is kicked up, then instantly sucked into the hole Superman left behind. Beat.

294   **EXT. OCEAN FLOOR - SAME TIME**   294

CRACK! Massive RIFTS appear in the ground around the crystal structure. Geysers of bubbles and gas explode from the crevices as the ocean floor is literally SPLIT OPEN.

294A   **INT. NEW KRYPTON - FORTRESS - SAME TIME**   294A

Lex's men are huddled together playing cards. Gazing at the other Kryptonian crystals, Lex clips a cigar -- triumphant. But just as he's about to light it:

> KITTY (O.S.)
> It's leaking.

He turns to see Kitty standing under her umbrella, shielding herself from small drops of water falling from the ceiling.

> LEX
> *Leaking*?
> (beat)
> Kitty -- I kill Superman and
> create all of this, and the only
> thing you can say to me is --
> "it's leaking"?

Beat. She looks at the Kryptonian crystals, wary.

> KITTY
> Are billions of people really
> going to die?

He lights the cigar.

> LEX
> Yes.

They suddenly feel the entire structure JOLT. Pieces of debris fall.

295   **EXT. NEW KRYPTON - SAME TIME**   295

Lex and the others exit the fortress and look around to see the horizon moving. They quickly realize the entire land mass is rising into the air. ONE OF THE MONOLITHS starts to crack.

> KITTY
> Lex, what's happening?!

THE MONOLITH cracks and tips over. Lex and the others scramble out of the way just as it CRASHES down onto the fortress.

> LEX
> Get to the helicopter! Now!

                         KITTY
               But our stuff--

                          LEX
               LEAVE IT! Leave everything!

A second monolith wavers and CRACKS. The thugs scramble to
get out of the way, and just as we think they're going to
make it -- it SMASHES directly on top of them. They're
GONE.

296   **INT. LEX'S HELICOPTER - SAME TIME**   296

Lex and Kitty climb into the helicopter.

                          LEX
               Here!

He hands her the case of crystals, freeing himself to start
the engines. She stares at the case with a look of
uncertainty and apprehension, which then becomes A MOMENT
OF DECISION.

With Lex distracted, Kitty quickly dumps the crystals out
the door. It *seems like* an accident.

Lex looks at her -- and at the crystals scattered outside.

                         KITTY
               Oops.

Infuriated, Lex is about to climb back out when he spots
CRACKS AND FISSURES forming under the chopper, threatening
to swallow them at any moment. They suddenly LURCH and
DROP. Too late.

297   **EXT. NEW KRYPTON - CANYON**   297

The ground under the chopper crumbles away, and it
disappears into a gaping chasm. Beat. VWROOOOM! A second
later, the helicopter comes flying out, safely soaring into
the sky.

298   **INT. LEX'S HELICOPTER**   298

Lex is staring out the window in a forlorn daze. Below, he
watches in horror as New Krypton rises out of the water.

299   **EXT. OCEAN SURFACE - SAME TIME**   299

Huge waves ripple outward as the land mass rises higher.
Its base finally breaks the surface, encased in a massive
chunk of brown, rocky, earth. We track along this stony
"root", until we find SUPERMAN -- a mere speck under the
massive structure, but managing to hold the entire thing
aloft.

300   **INT. SEA PLANE - SAME TIME**   300

LOIS, RICHARD, and JASON watch from the plane, stunned.

300A   **EXT. METROPOLIS COAST - SAME TIME**   300A

People on the coastline stare into the sky. From here, it
looks as if the giant mass is just FLOATING in mid-air.

300B   **OMITTED**   300B   *

301   **EXT. UNDER NEW KRYPTON - SAME TIME**   301   *

CLOSE ON: SUPERMAN, pushing it into the sky, summoning all
of his strength. This is the hardest thing he's ever done.

WIDER. Water cascades. Giant chunks of earth start to break
off, splashing into the ocean. As they do, something
strange becomes visible -- the faint glow of KRYPTONITE.

More rocks fall away, revealing deeper layers of
kryptonite. The glow becomes more intense, as bright as
what Superman saw in the remains of Krypton.

CLOSE ON SUPERMAN. He cringes, crying out in agony, almost
losing his grip, but he pushes higher into the storm
clouds.

303   **EXT. SPACE - OVER EARTH - CONTINUOUS**   303

MILES above Earth, Superman enters space, and with every
last bit of strength left, he lets out a PRIMAL SCREAM and
hurls New Krypton into space.

After a moment, Superman closes his eyes, and leans back.
But instead of flying back to Earth, we realize that he's
FALLING. Unconscious. Picking up speed, plummeting faster
and faster. VWOOSH! The air around him ignites BRIGHT
ORANGE.

304   **EXT. METROPOLIS, STREETS - MOMENTS LATER**   304

THE LIGHT illuminates the sky over the city. People point
and stare, terrified. A GLOWING STREAK tears through the
clouds.

305   **EXT. METROPOLIS PARK - CONTINUOUS**   305

...and CRASHES into a park. THE MASSIVE EXPLOSION knocks
over trees, and sends debris hundreds of feet into the air.

307   **EXT. METROPOLIS PARK - MOMENTS LATER**   307

It's quiet. Smoke and steam rise from the scorched crater.

308   **EXT. CRATER - MOMENTS LATER**   308

FROM WITHIN THE CRATER, we look up at its edge. Through the
smoke, we see A COP peering down. Another person joins him.
Then another. Soon the entire edge is filled with people.

               COP
        Oh my God...

FROM ABOVE

We see the crater in its entirety, and laying in its center
is SUPERMAN. Sprawled on his back. Body bruised. Not   *
moving. More people gather, staring down at their fallen
savior. A long, quiet beat before--

DOUBLE DOORS BURST OPEN.

309   **INT. METROPOLIS GENERAL - CORRIDOR - LATER**   309

TWO PARAMEDICS push a gurney followed by an escort of   *
POLICE. Like any man, our hero is being rushed into a   *
hospital. A DOCTOR and TWO NURSES hurry to meet them.   *

                    PARAMEDIC   *
          Breathing became shallow in   *
          transit. Can't get a blood   *
          pressure reading, but heart   *
          rate's less than thirty!   *

310   **INT. METROPOLIS GENERAL - TRAUMA ROOM - MOMENTS LATER**   310

A nurse tries to remove Superman's shirt. It won't come
off. The doctor reaches under his cape, near the shoulder.
And with a faint CLICK--   *

                    DOCTOR
          I think I got it.

--they remove the shirt, exposing his bare chest. The   *
doctor notices the STAB WOUND.   *

                    DOCTOR (CONT'D)   *
          Penetrating stab wound to right   *
          side of back. No hemorrhage.   *

The nurses attach EKGs. The line on the screen is flat.   *

                    NURSE   *
          Flatline!   *

                    DOCTOR   *
          Give him an epinephrine one
          milligram I.V. push!

The nurse tries to insert the NEEDLE into his arm. It
breaks.   *

                    DOCTOR (CONT'D)   *
          Shock at two-hundred!

                    NURSE
          Is that enough? He's not...
          human.

The doctor takes a breath, pauses... thinking...

189

                    DOCTOR
          Alright, charge to three-sixty...   *

THE DOCTOR places defibrillator paddles on Superman's
chest.

                    DOCTOR (CONT'D)
          Clear!

ZAP! THE PADDLES CRACKLE WITH ELECTRICITY. Lights flicker.
The defibrillator sparks and smokes, destroyed. Beat.   *

PUSH IN ON: The doctor, staring at the offscreen heart
monitor.

Silence, then... BEEP!

                                        SMASH CUT TO:

311   **SUPERMAN IS DEAD.**   311

The Daily Planet headline fills the frame. Beneath it is
Jimmy's photo of Superman holding up the Daily Planet
globe.

312   **INT. DAILY PLANET - PERRY'S OFFICE - THE NEXT DAY**   312

But it's just a printed mock-up. Perry looks it over. In
his other hand is ANOTHER MOCK-UP. It reads "SUPERMAN
LIVES". Richard looks at the headline, uneasy...

                         RICHARD
               It's kind of morbid, Perry.

                         PERRY
                    (solemn)
               Always be prepared.

Richard looks out to the bullpen -- at LOIS at her desk.

                    PERRY (CONT'D)
               How is she?

313   **INT. DAILY PLANET - BULLPEN - DAY**   313   *

Work crews are cleaning up debris. Other than TVs and
phones, there's little noise. Jason sits in a chair across
from Lois' desk. Her face is blank, emotionless. A DOCUMENT
is open on her screen, but it's blank. She looks up,
catches some of the staff staring. TVs are blaring:

                         TV #1
               ...still reeling from the shock
               of a geologic disturbance in the
               mid-Atlantic...

Lois closes her eyes, trying to shut out the noise and hold
back tears. A HAND gently touches her arm. It's Jason. Lois
smiles and tenderly hugs him.

Richard approaches. She tries hiding her tears.

                         RICHARD
               Lois?

                         LOIS
               Yeah?

                    RICHARD
          We can leave whenever you're
          ready. I mean, you don't have to
          be here.

                    LOIS
          Where else would I be?

Richard looks up at a nearby TV. Hinting. Lois looks up.

                    REPORTER (ON TV)
          ...the world waits as Superman
          remains in critical condition at
          Metropolis General. Police have
          surrounded the area--

                    RICHARD
          I could drive.

She looks at him, uncertain. Perry walks out of his office.

                    PERRY
          Gil, what's the story on that big
          chunk of whatever-it-was Superman
          pulled out of the ocean?

                    GIL
          Well, astronomers say it settled
          into orbit somewhere between Mars
          and Jupiter. Supposedly, it's
          laced with kryptonite and still   *
          growing.   *

                    PERRY
          But what are we calling it?

                    GIL
          Planet Ten...?   *

                    PERRY
          Well that's a terrible idea.
              (spots Lois)
          Lois, what do you think?

Beat. Lois looks at Richard. Considering. Finally, she
grabs her coat and takes Jason's hand. Ready to go.

                    LOIS
          I don't know, Perry. Call it...
          New Krypton.   *

                    PERRY
          New Krypton. Gil, run with it.   *
          Where are you two going?   *

                              LOIS
                    To the hospital.   *

                              GIL
                    Is that Krypton with a C-R-I?

          Jimmy walks by, taking off a jacket.   *

                              JIMMY
                    I'd be careful down there, Miss
                    Lane. It's a mad house.

314   **EXT. METROPOLIS GENERAL - DAY**   314

          THOUSANDS OF PEOPLE surround the hospital, overflowing into
          the street: fans, mourners, press, and cults of people
          DRESSED IN THE S. Candles have been lit. Prayers whispered.
          Cops try to keep things under control.

314A   **INT. CAR - DAY**   314A

          Lois, Richard, and Jason stare out at the throngs of
          people. The hospital is just ahead, but they're not moving.

                              RICHARD
                    So much for parking.

                              LOIS
                    It's okay. I can walk. Think I
                    can get in?

                              RICHARD
                    You're Lois Lane. They'll let you
                    in.

                              JASON
                    I want to go with Mommy.

          Beat. Lois looks to Richard. He nods. Richard can tell this
          isn't going to be easy for Lois, and hugs her tight.

                              RICHARD
                         (whispers)
                    We did everything we could.

          A tear falls from her eye.

                              RICHARD (CONT'D)
                    I'll be right here.

314B   **EXT. METROPOLIS GENERAL - MOMENTS LATER**   314B

          LOIS and JASON work their way through the crowd, towards
          the hospital entrance.

315   **INT. METROPOLIS GENERAL - CORRIDORS**   315   *

Lois and Jason walk down a long corridor with A DOCTOR.
The walk seems endless for her, but she does her best.   *
People stare as she passes. She's quite the celebrity.   *

Finally, they approach a reception area guarded by two   *
officers.

                              DOCTOR   *
                    This way, miss Lane.   *

She starts to move forward, but then realizes that the   *
doctor is gesturing to his right, to a simple hospital room *
door. Lois pauses for a moment, uncertain, and opens the   *
door.   *

316   **INT. METROPOLIS GENERAL - SUPERMAN'S ROOM**   316

They nervously step inside. She stares at the floor for a
moment, then looks up and almost gasps when she sees
SUPERMAN, laying in a hospital bed. Unconscious. Hooked up
only to a heart monitor. Lois tries to hold it together.

>   LOIS
>   Could we have a minute, alone?

>   DOCTOR
>   Of course.

He leaves. The door closes. Lois and Jason stand quietly   *
across from the bed, staring at Superman.   *

>   JASON
>   Is he going to get better?

>   LOIS
>   I don't know.

>   JASON
>   I want him to. I like him.

>   LOIS
>   Me too.

She steps closer, trying to find words. It's not easy.

>   LOIS (CONT'D)
>   Can... can you hear me? They say
>   sometimes when people are in...
>   Nevermind.

No answer. Just the beep of the heart monitor. Eyes
brimming with tears, Lois finally approaches his bedside.

>   LOIS (CONT'D)
>   There's something... something I
>   need to tell you.

Lois bends down and WHISPERS something into Superman's ear
that we cannot hear.

On the other side of a half-drawn curtain, Jason approaches
Superman's neatly folded suit and runs his fingers over the
emblem. He looks up.   *

PUSH IN ON: Jason, watching his mother divulge the biggest   *
secret of their lives. He doesn't know what she's saying,   *
but knows it is important.   *

Lois finishes whispering. Leans closer. Closer. Shuts her
eyes *and kisses him*. It's tender. Everything she
remembered.

She pulls away, tears streaming. She looks at the heart
monitor, maybe hoping the kiss would bring him back. But
there's no change. No magic awakening.

Overwhelmed, Lois wipes away her tears and stands up. She opens the curtains, then gently takes Jason's hand.

> LOIS (CONT'D)
> Come on, honey.

They start for the door, when Jason breaks free, toddles back to the bed, and kisses Superman on the forehead. Lois' heart breaks. Jason runs back, and they walk out the door.

317   **EXT. METROPOLIS GENERAL - MOMENTS LATER**   317

Lois and Jason walk out of the hospital and look over the sea of people-- all staring at HER. FLASH! A camera snaps their photo. MICROPHONES are shoved in her face. Reporters swarm.

> REPORTER #1
> Miss Lane, what did he look like?

> REPORTER #2
> Did he say anything? Is he going
> to make it?

The police clear a path for Lois and Jason. She passes a   *
familiar face in the crowd -- MARTHA KENT, standing with   *
BEN HUBBARD. Martha watches Lois leave, then anxiously   *
stares up at the hospital.   *

318   **EXT. ISLAND - SUNSET**   318

Waves wash over TWO PEDICURED FEET standing on a rocky beach. They belong to KITTY KOWALSKI. She stares out at the ocean. It's almost peaceful. Almost. A FURIOUS SHRIEK pierces the calm. It's Lex, angrily hurling a coconut into the water.

> KITTY
> Lex, we only have six of those.

> LEX
> Six? SIX?! I'd trade three
> hundred thousand coconuts and
> every drop of your blood for ONE
> QUART-- OF GASOLINE!

RACK FOCUS to the helicopter on the beach. It's not much, but Lex finally has his island. Kitty rolls her eyes, looks down at her feet. She has drawn a huge 'S' emblem in the sand. A large wave washes over it.

                         KITTY
          Lex?

                         LEX
          What, Kitty?

Lex turns, sees a worried look on her face.

                         KITTY
              I think the tide's coming in.

Lex closes his eyes, simmers with rage. Can it get any worse?

319   **INT. METROPOLIS HOSPITAL, CORRIDOR - NIGHT**   319

A NURSE doing her rounds walks down the guarded hallway. She approaches the door to Superman's room. A cop opens it.

320   **INT. METROPOLIS HOSPITAL, SUPERMAN'S ROOM - CONTINUOUS**   320

The nurse enters, glancing over a chart. She approaches Superman's bed, looks up, and freezes in her tracks. The bed is empty. She looks at the chair. The suit is gone.

The nurse rushes to the window and opens the blinds. The window is OPEN. She gasps.

321   **INT. LOIS LANE'S HOUSE - BEDROOM - PRE-DAWN**   321

A BEDSIDE CLOCK reads 5AM. Richard sleeps soundly, but the other side of the bed is empty.

322   **INT. LOIS LANE'S HOUSE - KITCHEN - SAME TIME**   322

Lois types on her laptop. Only the title can be seen:

              "WHY THE WORLD NEEDS SUPERMAN, by Lois Lane"

Overcome, Lois stops. She stares at A FRAMED PHOTO of her with Richard and Jason. Beat. Frustrated, she gets up.

323   **EXT. LOIS LANE'S HOUSE - BACK PORCH - MOMENTS LATER**   323

Lois puts a cigarette to her lips, flicks the lighter -- but the flame dies. She looks around, puzzled. Nothing. She's alone. She flicks the lighter again and the flame holds, but she stops -- thinks twice. Beat. She drops the cigarette, stomps it out.

324   **INT. LOIS LANE'S HOUSE - JASON'S ROOM - NIGHT**   324   *

JASON sleeps quietly in his room. There is a soft breeze,   *
and we can barely make out A FIGURE standing in the   *
shadows. It's almost ominous, until the figure steps into   *
the moonlight: *

Superman. Healed. Standing tall. He looks down at Jason for   *
a long moment, maybe thinking about what to say. Then, he   *
quietly approaches and kneels by the bed, watching the boy   *
sleeping soundly. Finally, the words come to him: *

                    SUPERMAN   *
          You will be different. You will   *
          sometimes feel like an outcast.   *
          But you will not be alone. You   *
          will never be alone.   *

They're the same words his father once said to him, long   *
ago.   *

                    SUPERMAN (CONT'D)   *
          You will make my strength your   *
          own, see my life through your   *
          eyes, as your life will be seen   *
          through mine. The son becomes the   *
          father, and the father... becomes   *
          the son.   *

Beat. Superman gently touches Jason's head, and the boy   *
starts to waken. His eyes flutter open, and he looks up.   *

Superman is gone. Jason sits up and turns to the window,   *
but only finds curtains blowing in the wind.   *

325   **EXT. LOIS LANE'S HOUSE - BACK PORCH - SAME TIME**   325

Lois looks up to see SUPERMAN, hovering over the water in
front of her. They gaze at each other.

                    SUPERMAN
          Thank you, Lois.

Tears well in her eyes, struggling for something to say.

                    SUPERMAN (CONT'D)
          It's alright.

It's what she's wanted and needed to hear for years.

Suddenly, Superman looks up at the house. Lois follows his
gaze and turns to see Jason watching them from the window.

Superman and Lois both look at him, then back to each
other.

                    LOIS   *
          Will we still see you... around?   *

>   SUPERMAN   *
>   I'm always around. Goodnight,   *
>   Lois.   *

She gently smiles, watching as Superman rises up and
disappears into the clouds.

326   **EXT. SPACE - DAWN**   326

In the tradition of films past, Superman flies into the
heavens. He smiles at us, then turns and soars toward the
sunrise. A magnificent dawn breaks, casting a warm glow
over the planet.

Our greatest protector is finally home.

                            THE END

SUPERMAN
R E T U R N S ™

A Selection of Storyboards

LEX GETS FUNDED

1

2

2.1

3

4

5

2₁

6

7

8

9

KNOCK KNOCK!!

4.

KNOCK KNOCK!!

10

KNOCK KNOCK!!

11

12

5

13

14

15

16

17

18

7.

19

20

20.1

8.

21

22

23

9,

24

25

26

27

214

11,

-KNOCK KNOCK!!-

28

29

30

12.

31

32

32.1

13

14,

36

37

38

15

40

40,1

40,2

17

40.3

40.4

THE BANK ROBBERY

B

CONT...

C

CONTINUE.....

D

PUSH IN ON HEAD.......

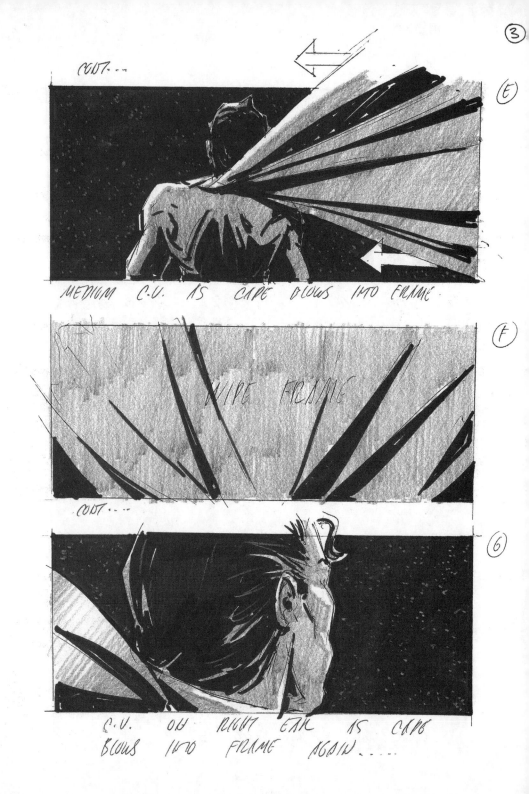

CONT...

MEDIUM C.U. AS CAPE BLOWS INTO FRAME.

WIPE FRAME

CONT...

C.U. ON RIGHT EAR AS CAPE
BLOWS INTO FRAME AGAIN.....

CONT.----

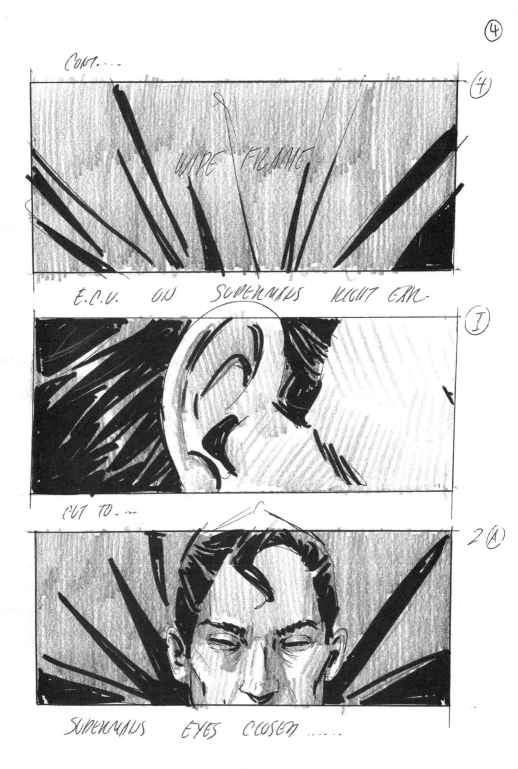

④

WIPE FRAME

E.C.U. ON SUPERMANS RIGHT EAR.

Ⅰ

CUT TO.--

2Ⓐ

SUPERMANS EYES CLOSED ......

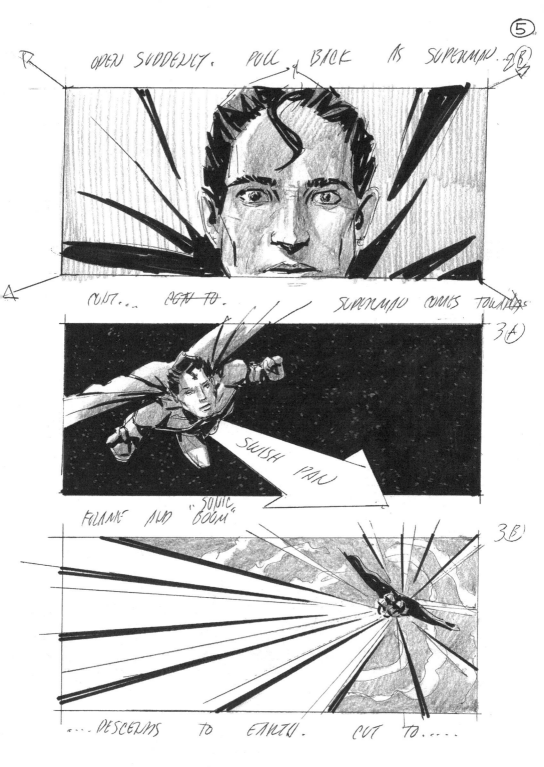

OPEN SUDDENLY. PULL BACK AS SUPERMAN. 2(B)

CUT... CGN TO. SUPERMAN COMES TOWARDS 3(A)

SWISH PAN

FLAME AND "SONIC BOOM" 3B

....DESCENDS TO EARTH. CUT TO.....

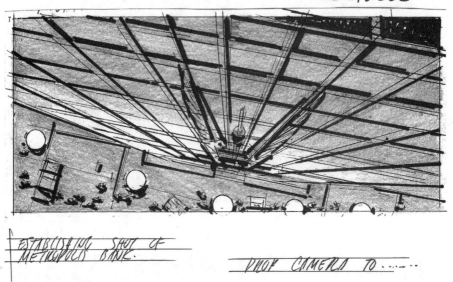

ESTABLISHING SHOT OF
METROPOLIS BANK.

DROP CAMERA TO ......

STREET LEVEL.
"YOU'RE SURROUNDED."

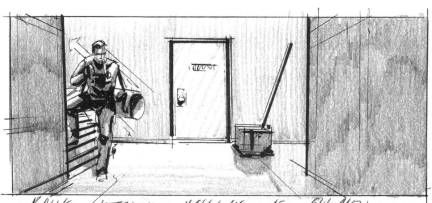

BANK INTERIOR HALLWAY AS GUNMEN
ASCEND STAIRCASE TO ROOFTOP. CUT TO.....
DOWNSHOT OF 2 GUNMEN

ESTABLISH 4 GUNMEN. CUT TO.....

REVERSE SHOWING OTHER TWO.

CUT TO ... BANK EXTERIOR. SPOTLIGHTS ON ROOF.

CUT TO ... INTERIOR HALLWAY WHERE GUNMEN
JUST WERE. PUSH IN ON ...... Ⓐ

JANITOR'S CLOSET AS ... DOOR SLOWLY OPENS Ⓑ

TO REVEAL ......

CONT----

2 SECURITY GUARDS AIMING INSIDE. (DIALOGUE)

CUT TO.---

SECURITY GUARDS ADVANCE UP TO
ROOFTOP SLOWLY. CUT. TO ...

(DIALOGUE) AS GUARDS REACH ANOTHER LEVEL.

(A)

(B)

CUT TO....

CUT TO. - ROOF TOP AS GUNMAN BREAK THROUGH DOOR Ⓐ ⑪

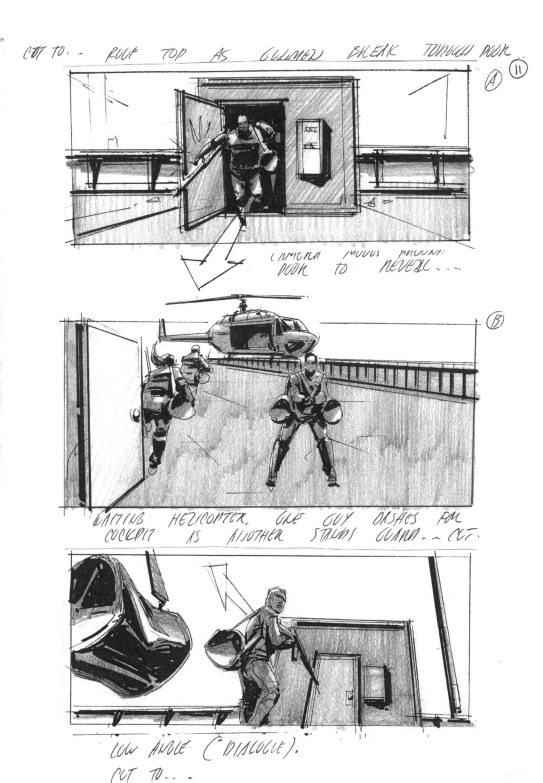

CAMERA MOVES AROUND
DOOR TO REVEAL...

Ⓑ

WAITING HELICOPTER. ONE GUY DASHES FOR
COCKPIT AS ANOTHER STANDS GUARD. - CUT.

LOW ANGLE (DIALOGUE).
CUT TO...

CUT TO.. SWAT ARMORED VEHICLE ARRIVES.

·DISTRIBUTE WEAPONS.

CUT TO.... GETTING READY FOR ASSAULT.

GROUND LEVEL AS POLICE MAKE WAY TO BLDG.
CUT TO... INTERIOR BLDG. AS GUARDS

CLIMB STAIRCASE. CUT TO...
GUARD TURNS ON WALKIE-TALKIE.

CUT TO...

SWAT CAPTAIN ON GROUND CALLING ON
FREQUENCY....

CUT TO... GUARDS INSIDE RESPOND.

CUT TO... DIALOGUE ON GROUND..

CUT TO...

CUT TO... GROUND LEVEL. TILT UP

1 GUNMAN STRIKES UP ROTOR.

CUT TO..... C.U. ROTOR

CUT TO...

GUNMAN 2 PULLS OUT RAIL FROM HELICOPTER.

FOLLOW HIM TO BUILDING'S EDGE---

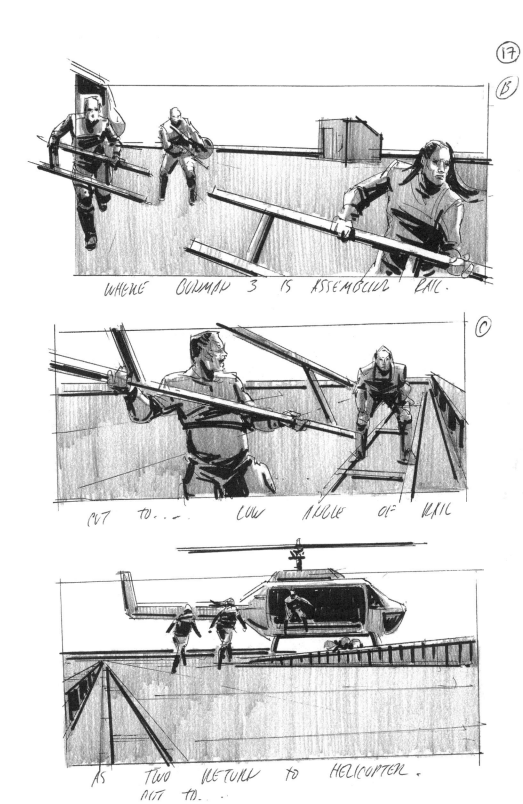

(B)

WHERE GUNMAN 3 IS ASSEMBLING RAIL.

(C)

CUT TO... LOW ANGLE OF RAIL

AS TWO RETURN TO HELICOPTER.
CUT TO...

INTERIOR OF HELICOPTER AS GUNMAN 4
PUSHES BIG GUN TOWARDS SLIDING DOOR.
CUT TO----

GUNMAN 2/3 CARRY GUN OUT WHILE GUNMAN 4 PUTS

MONEY INTO HELICOPTER.
CUT TO----

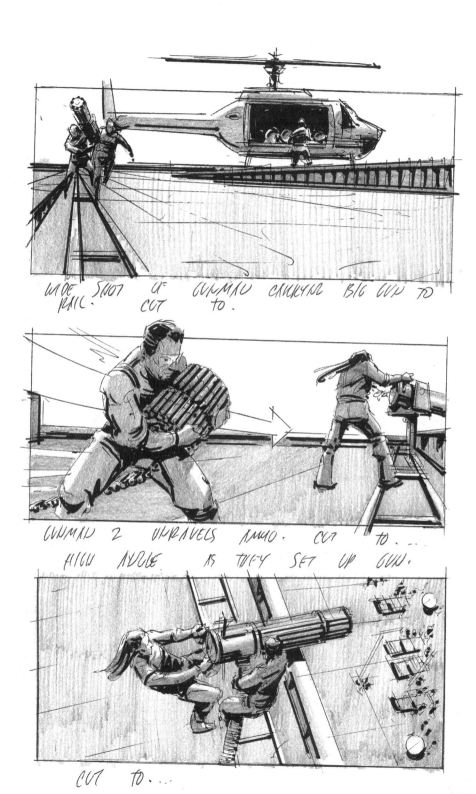

WIDE SHOT OF GUNMAN CARRYING BIG GUN TO RAIL. CUT TO.

GUNMAN 2 UNRAVELS AMMO. CUT TO.
HIGH ANGLE AS THEY SET UP GUN.

CUT TO...

LONG LENS AS GUN IS READY!

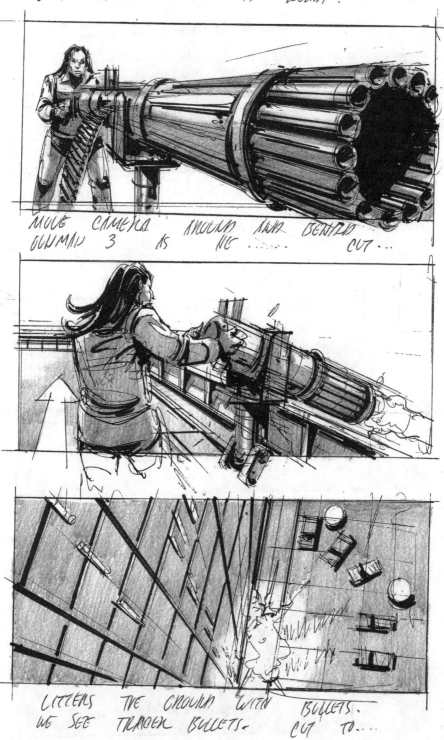

MOVE CAMERA AROUND AND BEHIND GUNMAN 3 AS HE .... CUT...

LITTERS THE GROUND WITH BULLETS.
WE SEE TRACER BULLETS. CUT TO....

GROUND LEVEL AS POLICE ARE OVERWHELMED.
CUT TO...

MONTAGE OF SPOTLIGHTS AND CARS... CUT

HIGH ANGLE OF SPOTLIGHTS BEING BLOWN OUT.
CUT TO...

GROUND LEVEL AS POLICE ASSAULT CONTINUES.

CUT TO POLICE RETREAT. CUT TO....

GROUND LEVEL AS CAMERA TILTS UP TO
TOP OF BLDG.

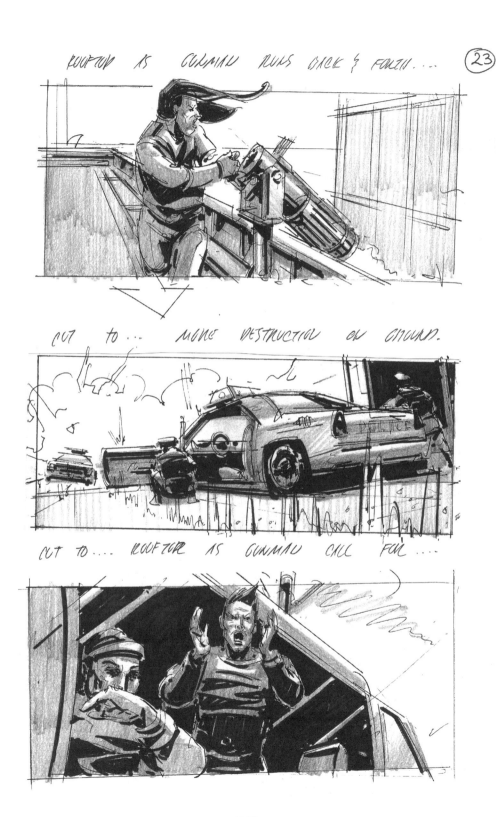

ROOFTOP AS GUNMAN RUNS BACK & FORTH .... (23)

CUT TO ... MORE DESTRUCTION ON GROUND.

CUT TO .... ROOFTOP AS GUNMAN CALL FOR ....

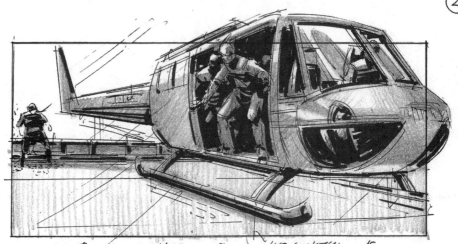

CUT TO.... M.S. OF HELICOPTER AS ....
CUT TO GUNMAN 3 IN A FRENZY...

CUT TO C.U. OF GUNMAN 3

CUT TO....

CUT TO.. ARMORED VEHICLE OVERTURNED

CUT TO.... MEN RETREAT

EVACUATE ARMORED TRANSPORT.

ROOFTOP DOORWAY. WINDY FROM ROTOR. CUT TO..

C.U. ROTOR. CUT TO....

INTERIOR, DOORWAY, AS SECURITY GUARDS GET READY.

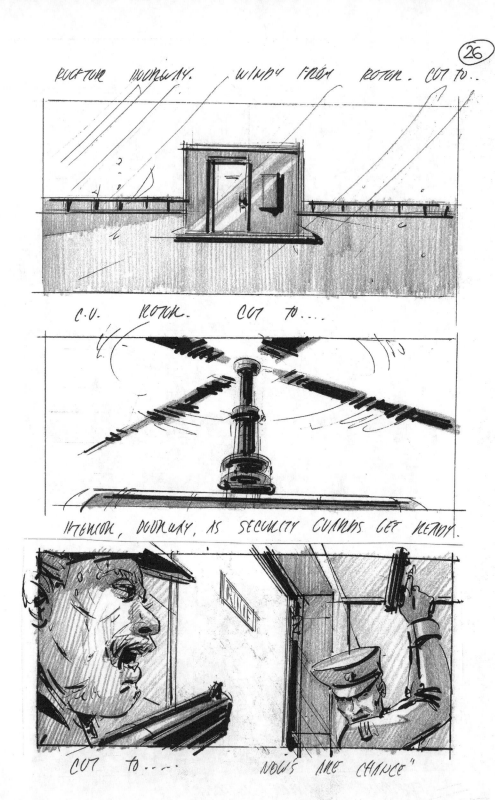

CUT TO..... "NOW'S THE CHANCE"

CUT TO GUNMAN 3 IN FOREGROUND.

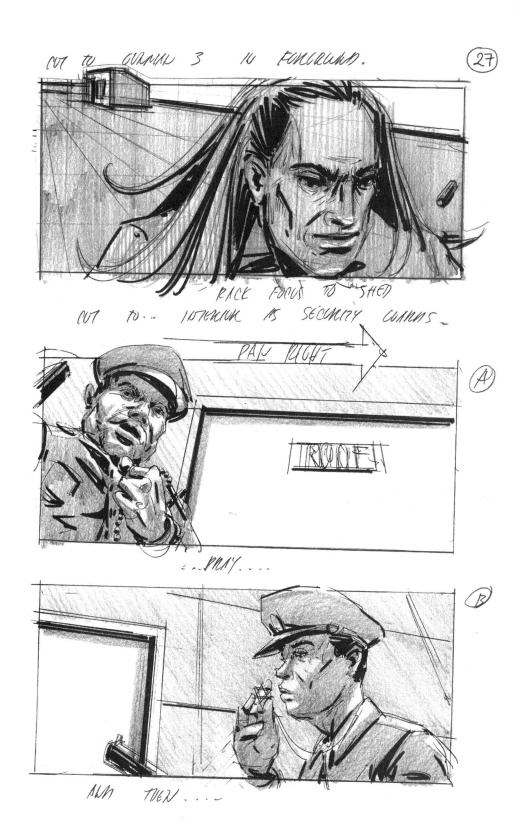

RACK FOCUS TO SHED

CUT TO... INTERIOR AS SECURITY GUARDS.

PAN RIGHT →

Ⓐ

...PRAY....

Ⓑ

AND THEN....

INTERIOR, STAIRCASE.
CUT TO LOW ANGLE AS
SECURITY GUARDS BURST THROUGH DOOR.

CUT TO.. EXT. AS GUARDS FIRE AND...

CUT TO... GUNMAN 3 HIT BUT WEARING
BULLETPROOF VEST.

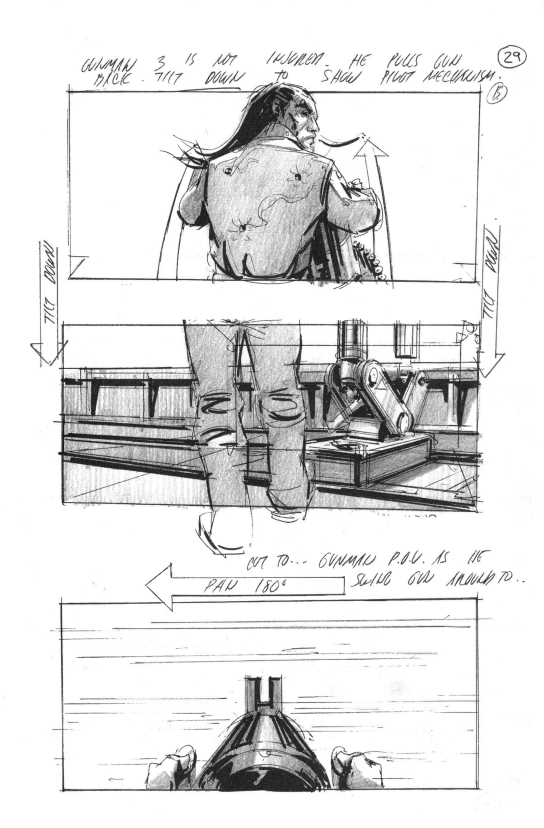

CONT....

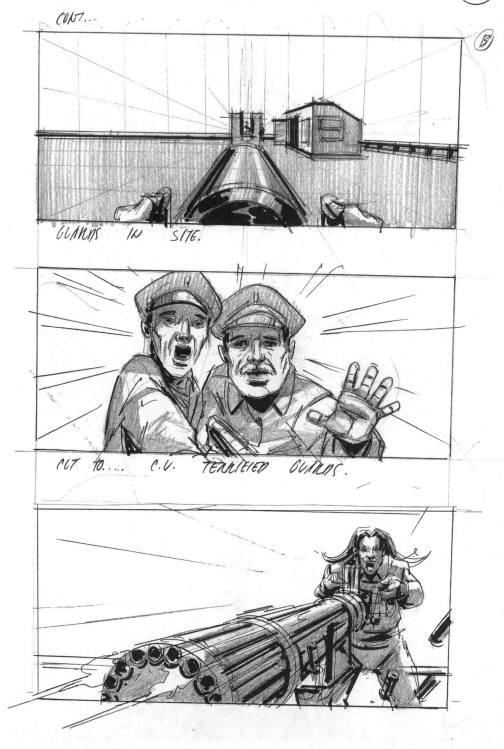

GUARDS IN SITE.

CUT TO..... C.U. TERRIFIED GUARDS.

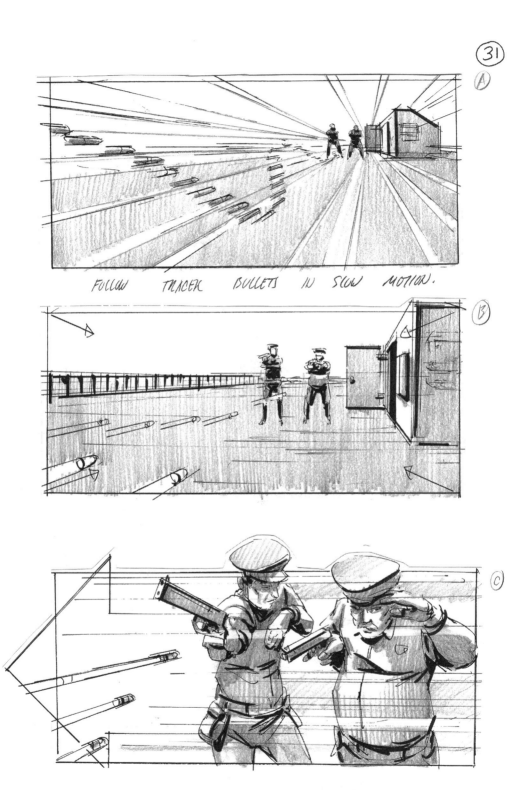

FOLLOW TRACER BULLETS IN SLOW MOTION.

REACTION SHOT OF GUARDS.

CUT TO... REACTION SHOT OF GUNMAN IN HELICOPTER.

CUT TO SUPERMAN WALKING TOWARDS CAMERA.

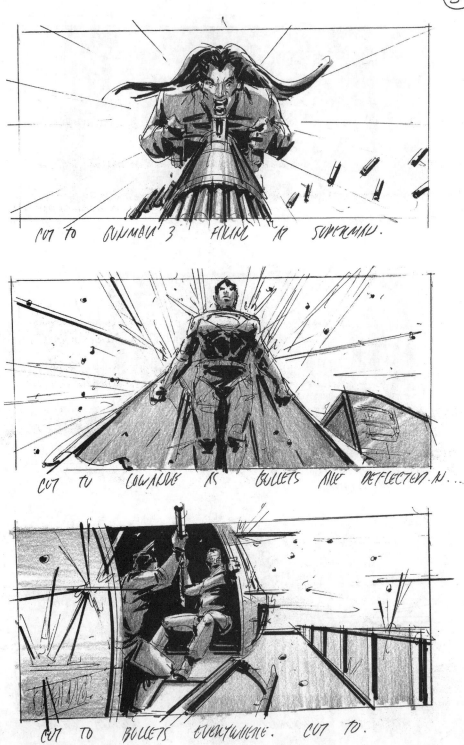

CUT TO GUNMAN'S FIRING AT SUPERMAN.

CUT TO COWARDS AS BULLETS ARE DEFLECTED IN....

CUT TO BULLETS EVERYWHERE. CUT TO.

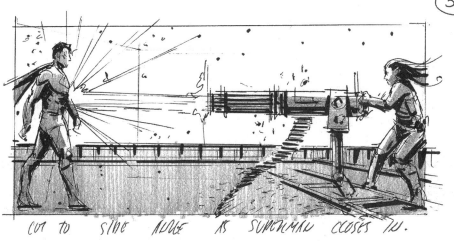

CUT TO SIDE ANGLE AS SUPERMAN CLOSES IN.

CUT TO... C.U. OF AMMO.

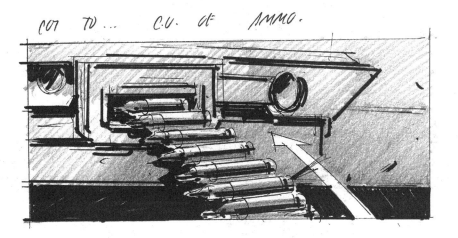

CUT TO ... SUPERMAN ADVANCING.

CUT TO.. C.U. OF AMMO DEPLETING.

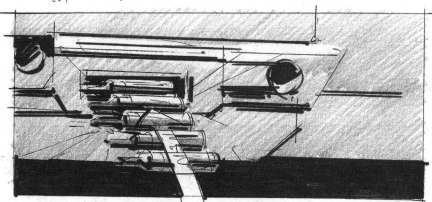

CUT TO... REACTION OF GUNMAN 3 AS

HE RUNS OUT OF AMMO.

DOLLY

CUT TO M.S. PAN LEFT TO.....

SUPERMAN IN FRONT OF GUN.

CUT TO... OVER SUPERMAN'S SHOULDER AS...

PAN LEFT

CUT TO... LOW ANGLE GUNMAN 3 PUSHES BIG GUN ASIDE. HE PULLS A MAGNUM OUT OF HOLSTER AND...

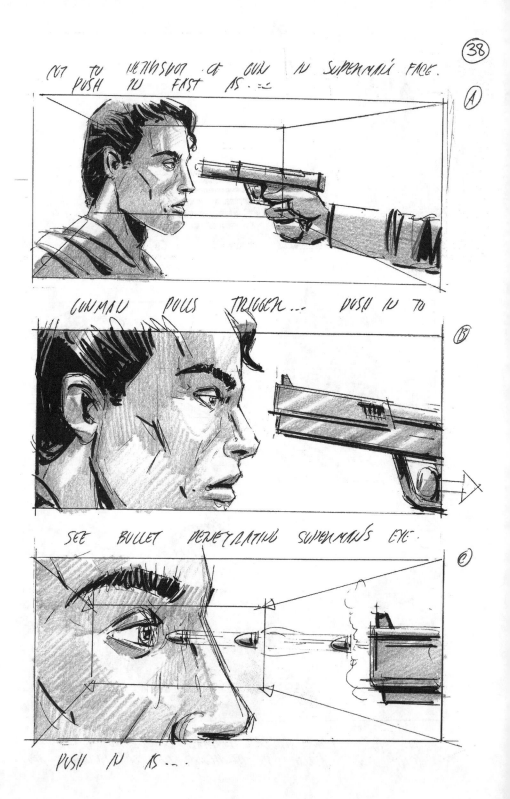

E.C.U. AS BULLET IMPACTS EYE AND...

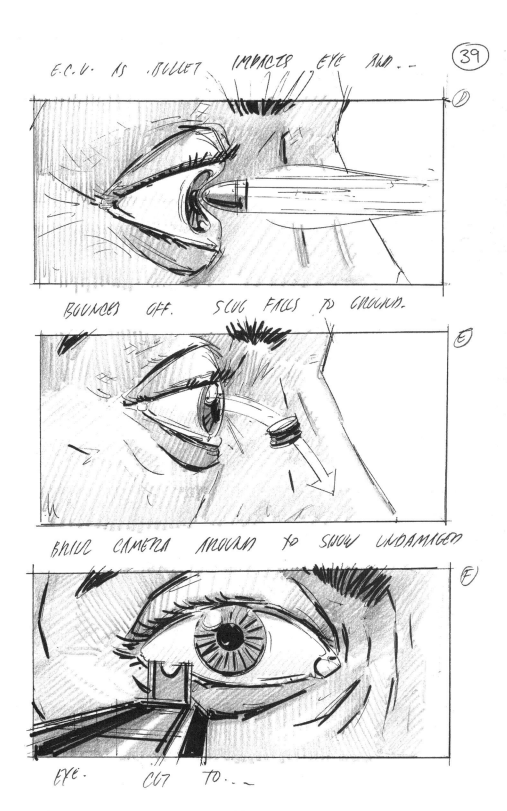

BOUNCES OFF. SLUG FALLS TO GROUND.

BRING CAMERA AROUND TO SHOW UNDAMAGED

EYE. CUT TO...

CUT TO.... OVER SUPERMAN'S SHOULDER. GUNMAN IS TERRIFIED. SUDDENLY, SUPERMAN IS HIT FROM BEHIND.

CUT TO... C.U. OF SHOTGUNSHELLS FALLING TO GROUND.

CUT TO SUPERMAN TURNS TO REMAINING GUNMEN.

CUT TO .....

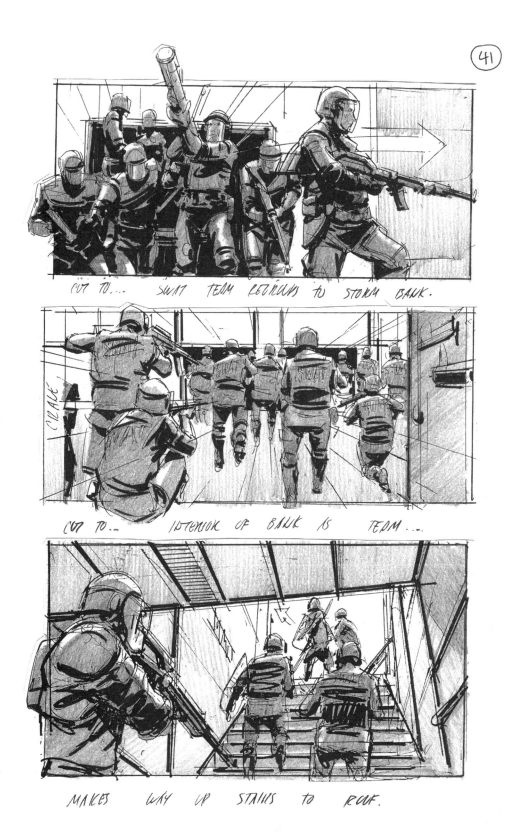

CUT TO.... SWAT TEAM REGROUPS TO STORM BANK.

CUT TO... INTERIOR OF BANK AS TEAM ...

MAKES WAY UP STAIRS TO ROOF.

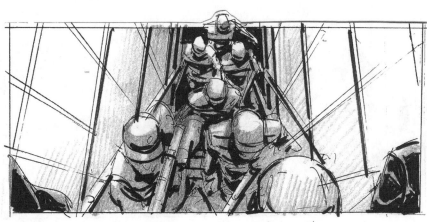

CUT TO DOWNSHOT FROM DOOR. CUT TO....

REVERSE ANGLE. PUSH THROUGH DOOR AS....

TEAM REACH ROOFTOP TO FIND AVIATION GUARDS.

CUT TO....   LOW ANGLE OF GUARDS

" WHAT TOOK YOU SO LONG?"

CUT TO... HIGH ANGLE , GUARDS AND   HELICOPTER

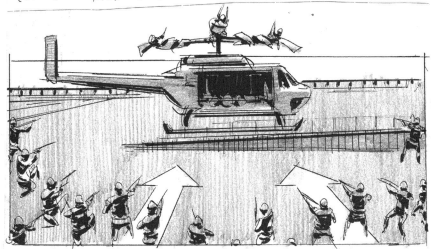

PULL   BACK   TO   REVEAL   SWAT TEAM.

CATCHING THE DAILY PLANET GLOBE